NATURAL TREATMENTS
For The World's
300
Most Common Ailments
PLUS

A Complete Guide
To
Vitamins - Minerals
Herbs - Essential Oils
Flower Remedies - Amino Acids
Tissue Salts & Other Essential
Natural Supplements

THIS GUIDE CONTAINS
REFERENCE INFORMATION ONLY
IT IS IN <u>NO WAY</u> INTENDED TO BE PRESCRIPTIVE OR DIAGNOSTIC.

Genesis 1: 29-30

"And God said, behold, I have given you every herb bearing seed, which is upon the face of all the earth, and every tree, in the which is the fruit of a tree yielding seed; to you it shall be for meat."

"And to every beast of the earth, and to every fowl of the air, and to everything that creepeth upon the earth, wherein there is life, I have given every green herb for meat: and it was so."

This book is a reference work based on extensive research. The intent is to offer natural alternatives for complex solutions to treat the breakdown of the immunity system. In the event you use this information without your doctor's approval, you are prescribing for yourself, which is your constitutional right, but the publisher and author assume no responsibility.

Global Health Ltd.
P.O. Box 419
Tofield, Alberta, Canada, T0B 4J0

Canadian Cataloguing in Publication Data
Nyholt, David Henry, 1940 – The vitamin and herb guide
Includes bibliographical references and index
ISBN 0-921202-24-5
1. Vitamin Therapy. 2. Herbs—Therapeutic use. I. Title
RM666.H33N94 2000 615'.321 C00-910744-4
Printed in United States of America

Dear Reader

This highly acclaimed international best selling guide has been completely revised and updated for the 21st century, providing the general public with the latest breakthroughs in vitamin and herb science. It is the most comprehensive, concise and straight forward natural health guide on the market today. Simplified, allowing you to skim through and find what you want and need to know when you're at your busiest, or digest at your leisure. Using the quick scan index, clearly designed charts on vitamins, minerals, herbs, amino acids and tissue salts, you get more information in less reading time. That's precisely why busy people like you around the world rely on the Vitamin & Herb Guide.

Global Health keeps you in touch with the proper natural treatments and remedies for the world's most common ailments. Also included, quick reference R.D.A. charts. Effects and side effects of the common vitamins, minerals, and herbs and in which foods they can be found. We are united in cause, to help you restore health, prevent premature aging, and prolong life. This guide will expand your awareness of treating yourself as naturally as possible, and discover a comfortable relationship with the latest natural alternatives for your busy lifestyle.

Global Health wishes to thank the following individuals for their time, energy, dedication and support in the preparation of the book.

Our sincere thanks to ...

Pearl Chapman	-	Research
Mark Ferguson	-	Research
Ann Brown	-	Research
Louise Kitura	-	Research
Gordon Ramsey	-	Research
Laura Rinas	-	Research
Betty Gervais	-	Research
Jim Patterson	-	Research
David Nyholt	-	Research, Editing
Joan Davis	-	Typesetting
Robert Lundquist	-	Cover Design, Artwork

Gordon Jones
Director, Global Health Research Foundation

Vitamin & Herb Guide...

INDEX

300 OF THE WORLD'S MOST COMMON AILMENTS

4

Vitamin & Herb Guide...
INDEX

VITAMINS
NATURAL OR SYNTHETIC 68

The Natural Choice...
INDEX

Vitamin & Herb Guide...
INDEX

INDEX

300 OF THE WORLDS MOST COMMON AILMENTS

ABSCESS . . . . .

SINGLE HERBS: Burdock Root, Cayenne, Echinacea, Red Clover, and Yellow Dock Root
VITAMINS: A multi-vitamin plus extra A, B complex, C, and E.
MINERALS: A mineral complex plus Zinc.
ESSENTIAL OILS: Bergamot, Garlic, Lavender, and Tea Tree.
FLOWER REMEDIES: Crabapple.
TISSUE SALTS: Ferr phos and Kali mur.
ALSO: Raw Thymus and Proteolytic enzymes.
REFERENCES:
The Complete Natural Health Encyclopedia - David Nyholt.

ACHILLES TENDINITIS . . . . .

HERBAL COMBINATION: (BF+C).
PHYSIOLOGIC ACTION: A special formula to aid in healing processes for swelling and inflammation.
SINGLE HERBS: White Oak Bark, Comfrey Root, Skullcap, and Yucca.
VITAMINS: B complex, B5, B6, B12, C, and E.
MINERALS: A Multi-mineral.
ESSENTIAL OILS: Birch, Geranium, Lavender, and Spearmint.
FLOWER REMEDIES: Take Bachs Rescue Remedy.
TISSUE SALTS: Ferr phos and Silicea.
REFERENCES:
The Complete Natural Health Encyclopedia - David Nyholt

10

The Athletes Bible - David Nyholt
The Fitness Formula - S. Sokol

ACNE . . . . .

HERBAL COMBINATION: AKN
PHYSIOLOGIC ACTION: Acne is nearly always the product of blood impurities. AKN helps cleanse toxins and mucus. Enhances overall good health and well-being, and helps eliminate skin blemishes and acne.
SINGLE HERBS: Burdock, Chaparral, Chlorophyll, Echinacea, Garlic, Gotu Kola, Red Clover, and Yellow Dock.
VITAMINS: A, B complex, B3, B6, C, E, and F.
MINERALS: Potassium and Sulfur.
ESSENTIAL OILS: Anise, Lemon, Chamomile, and Tea Tree oil.
FLOWER REMEDIES: Crabapple.
TISSUE SALTS: Calc phos, Kali mur, and Silicea.
ALSO: Primadophilus.
REFERENCES:
Acne - J. Howland
Global Herb Manual - Z. Fortisevn

AGING PREMATURE . .

SINGLE HERBS: Aloe Vera, Fo-ti, Ginger, Ginko Biloba, Ginseng, Gota Kola, and Milk Thistle.
VITAMINS: A complete multi-vitamin plus C, and E.
MINERALS: A multi-mineral plus Zinc
ESSENTIAL OILS: Garlic, Lemon, Onion, Thyme, and Spikenard.
FLOWER REMEDIES: Combine Aspen, Cherry Plum, Cerato, and Wild Oats.
TISSUE SALTS: Calc phos, Kali phos, and Nat mur.
ALSO: Coenzyme Q10.

REFERENCES:
The Complete Natural Health Encyclopedia - David Nyholt
Natural Treatments and Remedies - Global Health.

AIDS .....

(Acquired Immune Deficiency Syndrome)
SINGLE HERBS: Cayenne, Chinese Ginseng, Garlic, Milk Thistle, Pau d'Arco, Shiitake Mushroom, Sheep Sorrel, Suma, and Yucca.
VITAMINS: A, B6, B12 B complex (stress), and E.
MINERALS: High potency muli-mineral formula, plus Copper, and Zinc.
ESSENTIAL OILS: Bergamot, Neroli and Ylang-Ylang..
FLOWER REMEDIES: Take Bachs Rescue Remedy plus Mimulus.
ALSO: Canaid herbal drink, Acidophilus, Coenzyne Q10, Germanium, Gluconic from DaVinci Labs, Proteolytic Enzymes, Raw Thymus, and Multiglandulars.
REFERENCES:
Drugs and Beyond - David Nyholt
The Complete Natural Health Encyclopedia - David Nyholt.
Natural Treatments and Remedies - Global Health

AIR SICKNESS .....
Refer to *Motion Sickness* P 49

ALCOHOLISM .....

HERBAL COMBINATIONS:
(Thisilyn) (Milk Thistle) (PC) (Liveron) (AdrenAid).
PHYSIOLOGIC ACTION: The above herbal formulas support and rebuild the liver, pancreas, and adrenal glands. By supporting these systems, the taste for alcohol will eventually subside. The vitamin and mineral supplements strengthen the body's nutritional integrity to a state where the need for a "lift" will be eliminated.
SINGLE HERBS: Cayenne, Dande-lion, Siberian Ginseng, Golden Seal, Licorice Root, Lobelia, Nettle, Skullcap, and Valerian.
VITAMINS: A, B complex, C, D, and E.
MINERALS: Brewers Yeast, Magnesium and Zinc.
ESSENTIAL OILS: Chamomile, Clary Sage, and Fennel.
FLOWER REMEDIES: Impatiens.
TISSUE SALTS: Calc phos.
ALSO: Glutamine, and Tryptophan. Avoid meat and all refined and pro-cessed foods, especially white sugar and white flour.
REFERENCES:
Herbally Yours - P. Royal
Drugs and Beyond - David Nyholt
The Complete Natural Health Encyclopedia - David Nyholt.
How to get Well - P. Airola

ALLERGIES .....

HERBAL COMBINATION: (HAS: Original and Fast Acting Formulas) (AllergyCare)
PHYSIOLOGIC ACTION: HAS is an excellent formula which contains herbs that help relieve symptoms of hay fever, sinus congestion, chemical, and respiratory allergies. Helps drain nasal passages, relieve swollen membranes, eliminate mucus, and cleanse the body. The Fast Acting Formula adds Pseudoephedra, a natural plant extract from the Ephedra plant. This substance quickly opens nasal passages allowing free breathing. While HAS Fast Acting is not for prolonged use, HAS Original can be taken for as long as needed.

Caution: Both formulas are not to be used during pregnancy.

Allergy Care: Maximum-strength natural allergy medicine that will not cause drowsiness. It contains 60mg of the active ingredient Pseudo ephedrine Hcl.

Caution: Not to be used during pregnancy, nor by small children.

SINGLE HERBS: Burdock Root, Cayenne, Chaparral, Elderberry, Eyebright, Lobelia, Golden Rod, Golden Seal, and Nettle.

VITAMINS: A, B complex, B3, B5, B6, B12, C, E, and F.

MINERALS: Calcium, Magnesium, and Manganese.

ESSENTIAL OILS: Immortelle, Mellissa, and Yarrow.

FLOWER REMEDIES: Olive.

TISSUE SALTS: Kali phos and Mag phos.

ALSO: Bee Pollen, Propolis, and Digestive Enzymes.

REFERENCES:
Allergy - W. Crook
Every Woman's Book - P. Airola

ALOPECIA.....
Refer to *Baldness* Page 15

ALZHEIMERS.....

SPECIFICS: Excesses and deficiencies could be the key to the prevention or cure of Alzheimers. The herb Club Moss produces Huperzine which is considered to be the newest brain nutrient to enhance mental function and improve patients lives.

SINGLE HERBS: Club Moss, Butchers Broom, Kelp, and Ginkgo Biloba.

VITAMINS: B complex, plus B6, B12, C, and E.

MINERALS: Boron, Potassium, Selenium, Vanadium, and Zinc.

ESSENTIAL OILS: Basil and Rosemary.

FLOWER REMEDIES: Combine Chicory, Chestnut Bud, Heather, Holly, and White Chestnut.

TISSUE SALTS: Calc phos, Kali phos, and Nat mur.

ALSO: Coenzyme Q10, Lecithin, and Superoxide dismutase.

REFERENCES:
The Complete Natural Health Encyclopedia - David Nyholt.

AMNESIA.....

HERBAL COMBINATION: (SEN) or (Remem).

PHYSIOLOGIC ACTION: This formula contains remarkable rejuvenating properties that nourish the brain cells and tissues.

SINGLE HERBS: Cayenne, Ginkgo, Ginseng, Gotu Kola, and Lobelia.

VITAMINS: A, complete multivitamin complex plus Choline.

MINERALS: A complete multimineral complex..

ESSENTIAL OILS: Basil, Peppermint, and Rosemary.

FLOWER REMEDIES: Impatiens.

TISSUE SALTS: Nat sulph.

ALSO: Lecithine.

REFERENCES:
Mental Alertness - Donsbach
Vitamin Bible - E. Mindell

ANAL FISSURES.....
Refer to *Hemorrhoids* Page 38

ANEMIA.....
(Iron deficiency anemia)

SINGLE HERBS: Barley Grass, Beet Powder, Black Current, Chlorophyll, Chorella, Comfrey, Dandelion, Fenugreek, Kelp, and Yellowdock.

VITAMINS: A complete multivitamin and additional C.

MINERALS: Complete multi-mineral.
ESSENTIAL OILS: Lemon, Roman Chamomile, and Thyme.
FLOWER REMEDIES: Hornbeam.
TISSUE SALTS: Ferr phos.
ALSO: Dessicated liver.

ANGINA.....
Refer to *Myocardial Infraction* Page 50

ANXIETY.....
HERBAL COMBINATION: (Calm-aid) or (Ex stress comb).
PHYSIOLOGIC ACTION: This formula soothes, strengthens, and heals the whole nervous system. An excellent aid for insomnia, nervousness, and stress related conditions.
SINGLE HERBS: Evening Primrose Oil, Skullcap, and Yucca.
VITAMINS: B complex plus B1, B2, B3, B5, B6, and C.
MINERALS: Calcium, Iodine, Iron, Magnesium, Phosphorus, Potassium, Silicon, and Sodium.
ESSENTIAL OILS: Grapefruit, Marjoram, and Rose.
FLOWER REMEDIES: Take Bachs Rescue Remedy.
TISSUE SALTS: Calc phos, Kali phos, and Nat mur.
ALSO: Radish and prune juice.
REFERENCES:
Stress - Donsbach
Drugs and Beyond - David Nyholt
The Athletes Bible - Global
The Fitness Formula - S. Sokol

ARTERIOSCLEROSIS..
HERBAL COMBINATION:
(GARLICIN HC)
PHYSIOLOGIC ACTION: A combination of herbs which supports the cardiovascular system. Helps to strengthen the heart, while building and cleansing the arteries and veins.
SPECIFICS: Recent animal studies suggest that vitamin C deficiency could be involved in the causation of arteriosclerosis. E.F.A.s (essential fatty acids) play a fundamental role in keeping cell membranes fluid and flexible.
SINGLE HERBS: Cayenne, Comfrey, Evening Primrose Oil, Fish Oil, Garlic, Golden Seal, and Rose Hips.
VITAMINS: B complex, C, E, Niacin, Inositol, and Choline.
MINERALS: Calcium and Magnesium.
ESSENTIAL OILS: Cypress, Hyssop, and Thyme.
FLOWER REMEDIES: Impatiens.
TISSUE SALTS: Kali sulph.
ALSO: (E.F.A.s) — Fish oils and cold pressed vegetable oils.
REFERENCES:
Evening Primrose Oil - J. Graham
Fats and Oils - U. Erasmus

ARTHRITIS AND RHEUMATISM.....
HERBAL COMBINATION:
(Rheum-Aid) or (Yucca -AR)
PHYSIOLOGIC ACTION: Relieves symptoms associated with bursitis, calcification, gout, rheumatoid arthritis, rheumatism, and osteoarthritis. Helps the body reduce or eliminate swelling and inflammation in the joints and connective tissue and helps to relieve stiffness and pain.
SINGLE HERBS: Alfalfa, Black Cohosh, Burdock, Chaparral, Devil's Claw, and Yucca.
VITAMINS: Niacin, B, C, D, E, F, and P.
MINERALS: All.
ESSENTIAL OILS: Use Lavender, Pine, and Rosemary.

13

FLOWER REMEDIES: Aspen and Willow.

TISSUE SALTS: .Calc phos, Ferr phos, Kali sulph, and Nat phos.

ALSO: Cod liver oil, green magma, aqua life, seatone, bromelain, papaya, cherry juice, pineapple, goats milk, and mung beans.

REFERENCES:
There is a Cure for Arthritis
The Complete Natural Health Encyclopedia - David Nyholt.
How to Get Well - P. Airola

ASTHMA .....

HERBAL COMBINATIONS: (B R E) or (Breathe-Aid) and (ANTS Liquid Extract)

PHYSIOLOGIC ACTION: BRE or Breath-Aid effectively relieve symptoms associated with asthma, chest congestion and inflammation. Promotes free breathing, eliminates mucus and cleanses the body. ANTS Liquid Extract helps to relax bronchial spasms. It helps to cut mucus, and is helpful for chronic coughs.

SINGLE HERBS: Lobelia, Comfrey, Chlorophyll, Fenugreek, Mullein, and Nettle.

VITAMINS: A, B complex, B2, B3, B5, B6, B12, C, E, F, and Paba.

MINERALS: Manganese.

ESSENTIAL OILS: Benzoin, Cajeput, and Inula Graveolens.

FLOWER REMEDIES: Take Bachs Rescue Remedy.

TISSUE SALTS: Kali phos, Mag phos, and Nat mur.

ALSO: Bee Pollen, honey, (honey will aid in clearing mucus out of the lungs.) Garlic, juice fast, vegetarian diet.

REFERENCES:
How to Get Well - P. Airola
Nutrition Almanac - J. Kirschmann

Health Through God's Pharmacy - M. Treben

ATHLETES FOOT .....

SINGLE HERBS: Caprinex (caprylic acid) and Pau d'Arco.

VITAMINS: Vitamin C powder (crystals) applied directly to affected area helps fungus infestation.

ESSENTIAL OILS: Tea Tree Oil.

TISSUE SALTS: Kali sulph, Nat mur, and Silica.

ALSO: Keep dry and out of shoes until infection clears.

REFERENCES:
The Athletes Bible - David Nyholt
The Fitness Formula - S. Sokol

ATHLETIC INJURIES ..

HERBAL COMBINATION: (B F + C)

PHYSIOLOGIC ACTION: A special formula to aid in healing processes for torn cartilage's, sprained limbs, broken bones, multiple athletic injuries and associated swelling and inflammation.

SINGLE HERBS: White Oak Bark, Comfrey Root, Black Walnut Hulls, Lobelia and Skullcap.

VITAMINS AND MINERALS: A complete multi-one a day, (time released).

ESSENTIAL OILS: Marjoram.

FLOWER REMEDIES: Bachs Rescue Remedy.

TISSUE SALTS: Calc fluor, Ferr phos, Kali mur, and Kali sulph.

ALSO: Green-Lipped Mussel.

REFERENCES:
The Athletes Bible – David Nyholt
The Fitness Formula — S. Sokol

BACK PAIN .....

HERBAL COMBINATIONS: (Extress) (Kalmin Extract)

PHYSIOLOGIC ACTION: The herbs in these combinations help to relax muscles and reduce muscle tension. The Kalmin Extract has anti-spasmodic and anti-inflammatory qualities, which are helpful in back pain caused by muscle strain.

SINGLE HERBS: Licorice, Valerian, and White Willow Bark.

VITAMINS: Vitamin C and E.

MINERALS: Calcium, Magnesium, and Manganese.

ESSENTIAL OILS: Marjoram.

FLOWER REMEDIES: Take Bachs Rescue Remedy.

AMINOS: DL-Phenylalanine and L-Tryptophan.

REFERENCES:
How to Get Well - P. Airola
Global Herb Manual – Z. Fortisevn

BAD BREATH .....

SINGLE HERBS: Chlorophyll, Myrrh, Parsley, Peppermint, and Rosemary.

VITAMINS: A, B complex, B3, B6, C, and Paba.

MINERALS: Magnesium, and Zinc.

ESSENTIAL OILS: Eucalyptus.

TISSUE SALTS: Calc fluor, Ferr phos, and Mag phos.

ALSO: Primadophilus.

REFERENCES:
Vitamin Bible - E. Mindell
Halitosis - M. Crag

BALDNESS .....

SINGLE HERBS: Aloe Vera, Kelp, Primadophilus, Rosemary, Nettle, Yarrow, and Yucca

VITAMINS: A, B complex, B3, B5, B6, C, Biotin, Folic Acid, and Inositol.

MINERALS: Copper, Iodine, and Magnesium.

ESSENTIAL OILS: Birch, Clary Sage, Jojoba and Rosemary.

ALSO: L-Cysteine, L-Methionine, Protein, and Raw Thymus Glandular.

REFERENCES:
Stop Hair Loss - P. Airola
The Complete Natural Health Encyclopedia - David Nyholt

BEDSORES .....

HERBAL COMBINATION: (X-itch ointment) or (Derm-Aid ointment).

PHYSIOLOGIC ACTION: These formulas have a drawing and healing effect on tough to heal sores.

SINGLE HERBS: Goldenseal, Myrrh gum, and Pau d Arco.

VITAMINS: A, B complex, C, D, and E.

MINERALS: Copper Calcium, Magnesium, and Zinc.

ESSENTIAL OILS: Geranium, Inula, and Rose.

TISSUE SALTS: Ferr phos and Kali phos.

BED WETTING .....
Refer to *Incontinence* Page 42

BEE STINGS .....

SINGLE HERBS: Echinacea, Pau d'Arco, and Yellow Dock Tea.

VITAMINS: B1 is a good insect re-pellent, and it creates a smell at the level of skin, that insects do not like. C — if already stung, use vitamin C to ease allergic reaction (acts as a natural antihistamine).

MINERALS: Calcium.

ESSENTIAL OILS: Tea Tree Oil.

FLOWER REMEDIES: Take Bachs Rescue Remedy.

TISSUE SALTS: Nat mur.

REFERENCES:
The Complete Natural Health Encyclopedia - David Nyholt
Natural Treatments and Remedies - Global Health

Vitamin & Herb Guide...

BELCHING .....
Refer to *Gas Intestinal* Page 34

BLADDER CANCER ....
Refer to *Cancer* Page 21

BLADDER IRRITABLE.
Refer to *Kidney & Bladder* P 43

BLEEDING GUMS .....
Refer to *Teeth & Gums* Page 62

BLOOD CLEANSER ....
HERBAL COMBINATION: (Red Clover Combination)
PHYSIOLOGIC ACTION: Helps cleanse the blood of toxins, mucus, and infections thus helps improve and sustain overall good health; used for many years with very good results.
SINGLE HERBS: Red Clover, Chaparral, Dandelion, Garlic, and Burdock.
MINERALS: Iron.
ESSENTIAL OILS: Eucalyptus.
TISSUE SALTS: Silicea.
ALSO: Chlorophyll and Diulaxa tea.
REFERENCES:
Herbally Yours - P. Royal
The Herb Book - J. Lust
Vitamin Bible - E. Mindell

BLOOD CLOTS .....
HERBAL COMBINATIONS: (Garlicin HC)
PHYSIOLOGIC ACTION: A combination of herbs that help strengthen the heart while building and cleansing the arteries and veins.
SINGLE HERBS: Comfrey, Garlic, Golden Seal, Kelp, and Rose Hips.
VITAMINS: B complex (stress) C, E, Inositol, Choline, and Niacin.

MINERALS: Calcium, Magnesium, and Selenium.
ESSENTIAL OILS: Lemon.
FLOWER REMEDIES: Take Bachs Rescue Remedy.
ALSO: Evening Primrose Oil and Fish Oil.
REFERENCES:
Herbally Yours - P. Royal
Blood Pressure - Donsbach
The Complete Natural Health Encyclopedia" - David Nyholt
Natural Treatments and Remedies - Global Health

BLOOD PRESSURE (HIGH) .....
HERBAL COMBINATION: (BP) (Cayenne-Garlic) (Garlicin HC)
PHYSIOLOGIC ACTION: BP improves overall blood circulation and tends to normalize high or low pressure to the body's normal level. Cayenne-Garlic and Garlicin HC lower blood pressure.
SINGLE HERBS: Cayenne, Garlic, Hawthorn, Kelp, Mistletoe, Valerian Root, and Yarrow.
VITAMINS: A, B Complex, B3, B5, B15, C, D, E, P, Inositol, Choline, and Lecithin.
MINERALS: Calcium, Magnesium, and Potassium.
ESSENTIAL OILS: Lavender, Marjoram, Melisa, and Nutmeg.
FLOWER REMEDIES: Take Bachs Rescue Remedy.
TISSUE SALTS: Calc fluor.
REFERENCES:
Herbally Yours - P. Royal
The Complete Natural Health Encyclopedia - David Nyholt
Global Herb Manual - Fortisevn

BLOOD PRESSURE (LOW) .....
HERBAL COMBINATION: (B/P)

16

PHYSIOLOGIC ACTION: A time proven formula that improves overall blood circulation and tends to normalize high or low pressure to the body's normal level. Also reduces cholesterol build-up in the blood vessels. Helps relieve symptoms of cold and flu.

SINGLE HERBS: Garlic, Hawthorn, Siberian Ginseng, Kelp, Golden Seal Root, Ginger Root, and Spirulina,

VITAMINS: A, B Complex, B5, C, E, P, and Lecithin.

ESSENTIAL OILS: .Clary sage.

TISSUE SALTS: Calc phos, Kali phos, Nat mur, and Silica.

ALSO: EPA. and Salmon oil.

REFERENCES:
Herbally Yours - P. Royal
The Complete Natural Health Encyclopedia - David Nyholt.
Vitamin Bible - E. Mindell
Nutrition Almanac - J. Kirschmann

BLOOD PURIFIER .....

HERBAL COMBINATION: (Red Clover Combination)

PHYSIOLOGIC ACTION: This combination effectively aids the body's cleansing systems, especially the bloodstream. Should be included as a nutritional supplement in all chronic or degenerative conditions. Can be used with most detoxification programs.

SINGLE HERBS: Alfafa, Alfamax, Burdock, Chaparral, Echinacea, Devils Claw, Oregon Grape Root, Pau d' Arco, Red Clover, and Yellow Dock.

MINERALS: Iron, and Germanium.

REFERENCES:
Herbally Yours - P. Royal
Health Through God's Pharmacy - M. Treben

BOILS .....

HERBAL COMBINATION: (AKN)

PHYSIOLOGIC ACTION: Many skin diseases are often related to liver dysfunction. This herbal formula combines herbs which support the liver, and clean the blood.

FOR PAIN: Make a paste of wheat flour and honey, spread over area, and cover with cotton dressing.

SINGLE HERBS: Chaparral, Dandelion, Echinacea, Lobelia, Mullein, and Red Clover.

VITAMINS: A, C, E. Vitamin A may be applied locally.

MINERALS: Zinc (preventative).

ESSENTIAL OILS: Tea Tree oil.

TISSUE SALTS: Ferr phos, Kali mur, and Silica.

REFERENCES:
Natural Treatments and Remedies - Global Health
Health Through God's Pharmacy - M. Treben

BONE, FLESH, AND CARTILAGE .....

HERBAL COMBINATION: (BF + C)

PHYSIOLOGIC ACTION: A special formula to aid the body's healing processes involved with broken bones, athletic injuries, sprained limbs, and related inflammation and swelling. A tonic used after acute and chronic diseases to help rebuild the body.

SINGLE HERBS: Comfrey Root, Black Walnut, Lobelia, Skullcap, and White Oak Bark.

VITAMINS: A, C, and D.

MINERALS: Calcium, and Magnesium.

FLOWER REMEDIES: Take Bachs Rescue Remedy.

TISSUE SALTS: Calc fluor, Ferr phos, Kali mur, and Kali sulph.

NOTE: Vitamin C and Calcium accelerate bone healing.

REFERENCES:
The Athletes Bible – David Nyholt
The Fitness Formula - S. Sokol

BONE SPUR....
Refer to *Heel Spur* **Page 38**

BOWEL CLEANSER....
HERBAL COMBINATION:
(Multilax #2) or (Naturalax #2)

PHYSIOLOGIC ACTION: Accelerates natural cleansing of the body and improves intestinal absorption by gentle evacuation of the bowels. It cleans out old, toxic fecal matter, mucus and encrustation's from the colon wall, and helps normalize the peristaltic action and rebuild the bowel structure. Use until the bowel is cleansed, healed, and functioning normally.

Warning: Do not take during pregnancy.

SINGLE HERBS: Cascara Sagrada, Golden Seal Root, Lobelia, Red Raspberry, and Senna.

VITAMINS: B complex.

TISSUE SALTS: Mag phos, Nat mur, Nat phos, and Silicea.

ALSO: Flax seeds, Psyllium seeds, Whey Powder, Brewers Yeast, Yogurt, soaked Prunes and Figs, and Licorice tea.

REFERENCES:
Colon Health - Walker
How to Get Well - P. Airola

BREAST CANCER.....
Refer to *Cancer* **Page 21**

BREAST FEEDING....
SINGLE HERBS: Alfalfa, Blessed Thistle, Chlorophyll, Fennel, Red Raspberry, or Marshmallow (warm) will bring in good rich milk. Sage will help dry up the milk when the mother is ready to quit nursing.

VITAMINS: If baby has a cold, mother can take extra vitamin C.

ESSENTIAL OILS: Anise, Fennel, and Jasmine oil increase milk production.

TISSUE SALTS: Calc phos.

CAUTION: A nursing mother should not take cleansing herbs as it may cause colic or diarrhea in the baby.

REFERENCES:
The Complete Natural Health Encyclopedia - David Nyholt.
Herbally Yours - P. Royal

BREATHING DIFFICULTIES.....
HERBAL COMBINATIONS: (B R E) or (Breathe-Aid) (Fenu-Comf)

PHYSIOLOGIC ACTION: Effectively relieves irritation and promotes healing throughout the respiratory tract. Eliminates mucus, inflammation of the lungs, and helps relieve symptoms of coughs, colds, and bronchitis.

SINGLE HERBS: Comfrey Leaves, Lobelia, Marshmallow Root, and Mullein.

VITAMINS: C.

ESSENTIAL OILS: Benzoin, Cajeput, and Inula Graveolens.

FLOWER REMEDIES: Take Bachs Rescue Remedy.

TISSUE SALTS: Ferr phos and Kali mur.

ALSO: Respa-Herb and Bee Pollen.

REFERENCES:
Health Through God's Pharmacy - M. Treben

BRIGHTS DISEASE....

HERBAL COMBINATION: (KB)
PHYSIOLOGIC ACTION:
Extremely valuable in healing and strengthening the kidneys, bladder, and genito-urinary area.
SINGLE HERBS: Alfalfa, Barberry Root, Catnip, Dandelion, Fennel, Ginger Root, Horstail, and Wild Yam..
VITAMINS: A, B complex, C, D, E, and Choline.
ESSENTIAL OILS: Bergamot, Tea Tree, and Thyme.
FLOWER REMEDIES: Take Bachs Rescue Remedy.
TISSUE SALTS: Ferr phos, Kali mur, and Silicea.
ALSO: Cranberry Juice, Propolis, Uratonic, and 3-Way Herb Teas.
REFERENCES:
The Complete Natural Health Encyclopedia - David Nyholt
Natural Treatments and Remedies - Global Health

BROKEN BONE....

Refer to *Fracture* Page 34

BRONCHITIS.....

HERBAL COMBINATION: (Fenu-Comf)
PHYSIOLOGIC ACTION: Helps relieve symptoms of coughs, colds, bronchitis, and helps eliminate mucus, congestion and inflammation from the lungs.
SINGLE HERBS: Comfrey, Eucalyptus, Lobelia, Chickweed Tea, Slippery Elm. Cayenne taken with Ginger cleans out the bronchial tubes.
VITAMINS: A, B12, C, and E.

MINERALS: A multi-mineral plus Zinc.
ESSENTIAL OILS: Eucalyptus, Lemon, Sandalwood, and Thyme.
TISSUE SALTS: Ferr phos, Kali mur, and Kali sulph.
ALSO: Acidophilus-Liquid.
REFERENCES:
Herbally Yours - P. Royal

BRUXISM.....
Refer to *Teeth Grinding* Page 62

BUNION.....

SINGLE HERBS: Caster, Chamomile, Flaxseed, and Termeric.
VITAMINS: A complete multivitamin.
MINERALS: A complete multimineral.
ESSENTIAL OILS: Lavender, Lemon Balm, Orange, and Thyme.
FLOWER REMEDIES: Holly and White Chestnut.
TISSUE SALTS: Silicea.
ALSO: Pine bark and Grapeseed extracts.
REFERENCES:
The Complete Natural Health Encyclopedia - David Nyholt

BURNING FEET.....

VITAMINS: B6.
MINERALS: Iron.
REFERENCES:
How to Get Well - P. Airola

BURNS.....

SINGLE HERBS: Aloe Vera, and Comfrey.
PHYSIOLOGIC ACTION: Aloe Vera is very good for burns, it may be used internally and externally. Some Aloe Vera preparations contain lanolin, which will intensify burns. Use a preparation without lanolin. Aloe Vera is especially good for acid burns.

VITAMINS: C, E, Paba. (Vit E applied directly to burn). Take vitamin C hourly-this may prevent infection from occurring.
MINERALS: Zinc.
ESSENTIAL OILS: Chamomile, Geranium, and Tea Tree Oil.
FLOWER REMEDIES: Take Bachs Rescue Remedy.
TISSUE SALTS: Calc sulph, Ferr phos, and Kali mur.
ALSO: Ice, cold water, Paba cream, liquid honey, and Comfrey poultice.
REFERENCES:
Herbally Yours - P. Royal
Aloe Vera Handbook - M. Skousen
Nutrition Almanac - J. Kirshmann
How to Get Well - P. Airola

BURSITIS . . . . .
HERBAL COMBINATIONS:
(Rheum-Aid) (Cal-Silica) (Kalmin)
PHYSIOLOGIC ACTIONS: These herbal combinations contain herbs which exhibit anti-inflammatory and relaxing effects. Help to build nerve tissue, and relieve stiffness and pain.
SINGLE HERBS: Alfalfa, Chaparral, Comfrey. Mullein is often used as a poultice to give relief externally.
VITAMINS: A, B12, B Complex, C, E, and P.
MINERALS: Calcium and Magnesium.
ESSENTIAL OILS: Cajeput, Juniper, Rosemary, and Thyme.
FLOWER REMEDIES: Impatiens.
TISSUE SALTS: Silica.
ALSO: Peanut oil, and Alkaline diet.
REFERENCES:
Herbally Yours - P. Royal
Vitamin Bible - E. Mindel

CALAMYDIA . . . . .
SINGLE HERBS: Echinacea, Golden Seal, Pau d' Arco, Red Clover, and Suma.
VITAMINS: A, B complex, and K.
MINERALS: Zinc.
ESSENTIAL OILS: Neroli and Niaouli.
FLOWER REMEDIES: Combine Holly, Hornbeam, Impatiens, and White Chestnut.
TISSUE SALTS: Ferr phos, Kali phos, and Nat mur.
ALSO: Acidophilus, Coenzyme Q10, Germanium, and Protein.
REFERENCES:
Drugs and Beyond - David Nyholt
The Complete Natural Health Encyclopedia - David Nyholt

CALCIUM DEFICIENCY
HERBAL COMBINATION: Ca -T
PHYSIOLOGIC ACTION: This proven formula contains organic calcium, Silica and other tranquilizing minerals help prevent cramps. A natural way to calm nerves and aid sleep in addition to rebuilding the nerve sheath, vein, artery walls, teeth, and bones.
SINGLE HERBS: Comfrey Root, Horsetail, and Lobelia.
VITAMINS: D.
MINERALS: Calcium, Fem-Cal.
ALSO: Dark green leafy vegetables such as kale, mustard greens, collard greens, cabbage, broccoli, are rich sources of easily assimilated calcium. Foods such as lentils, almonds, and sesame seeds are other good sources.
REFERENCES:
Calcium Bible - P. Hausman
Health Through God's Pharmacy - M. Treben

CALCULUS .....
Refer to *Kidney and Bladder Stones* Page 44

CANCER .....
HERBAL COMBINATION: (Red Clover Combination)
PHYSIOLOGIC ACTION: This herbal combination contains herbs that are very similar to the Hoxey formula used to treat cancer. It is unique in that it cleanses and feeds the body.

Canaid herbal drink is similar, in nature and properties, to the famous Essiac treatment that has supposedly cured thousands of terminal patients.

The herb Pau d' Arco possesses antibiotic, tumor inhibiting, virus killing, anti-fungal and anti-malarial properties. Red clover, burdock and chaparral act as blood cleansers.

SINGLE HERBS: Bloodroot, Buckthorn Bark, Burdock, Chaparral, Cleavers, Garlic, Ginger, Ginseng, Golden Seal, Liquid Echinacea Extract, Pau d' Arco, Red Clover, Suma, Violet Leaves, and Yucca.
ESSENTIAL OILS: Basil, Elemi, Germanium, Hyssop, Tarragon, Tea Tree, Thuja, and Violet.
FLOWER REMEDIES: Take Bachs Rescue Remedy.
TISSUE SALTS: Calc phos, Kali phos, and Silicea.
ALSO: There are various Chinese herbs which have been used successfully while treating cancer, Some of these herbs include: Reishi Mushroom, Astragalus, Ligustrum, Codonopsis, and Schizandra.
Research indicates that pancreatic and other enzymes are a vital part of a cancer program. It has also been noted that potassium is vital.

Along with all the supplements, coffee enemas are important to cleanse the system and stimulate liver function.
VITAMINS: A, B3, B complex, C, E, Beta Carotene, and Digestive Enzymes.
MINERALS: Germanium, Magnesium, Potassium, and Selenium.
ALSO: Almonds, Apricot Pits, Red Beet Juice, Liver Extract, Brewers Yeast, Raw Food, Low Animal Protein, and Green Juices.
REFERENCES:
The Complete Natural Health Encyclopedia - David Nyholt
Cancer, the Total Approach - P. Airola
Killing Cancer - J. Winters
Second Opinion - B. Weed

CANDIDA ALBICANS ..
HERBAL COMBINATION: (Cantrol)
PHYSIOLOGIC ACTION: An excellent well balanced formula of herbs and supplements which balance the system while killing yeast. It includes caprylic acid and anti-oxidants for the control and eventual elimination of candida overgrowth.
SINGLE HERBS: Black Walnut, Caprinex, Garlicin, and Pau d'Arco.
VITAMINS: Biotin
ESSENTIAL OILS: Tea Tree Oil.
FLOWER REMEDIES: Combine Holy, Impatiens, and White Chestnut.
TISSUE SALTS: Calc phos, Kali phos, and Nat mur.
ALSO: Linseed Oil, Candida Cleanse, Caprilic Acid, Primodophilus
REFERENCES:
The Yeast Connection - W. Crook
Candida Albicans - L. Chaitow
Candida Cookbook - S. Rockwell

CANKER SORES.....

SINGLE HERBS: Burdock root tea, Goldenseal, and Pau d'Arco.
VITAMINS: A, B5, B12, B Complex, and large doses of C.
MINERALS: Iron.
ESSENTIAL OILS: Bergamot.
TISSUE SALTS: Cali phos and Nat mur.
ALSO: Avoid sugar and citrus fruits.

CARBUNCLES.....

HERBAL COMBINATION: (AKN)
PHYSIOLOGIC ACTION: Many skin diseases are often related to liver dysfunction. This herbal formula combines herbs which support the liver, and clean the blood.
FOR PAIN: Make a paste of wheat flour and honey, spread over area, and cover with cotton dressing.
SINGLE HERBS: Chaparral, Dandelion, Echinacea, Lobelia, Mullein, and Red Clover.
VITAMINS: A, C, E. Vitamin A may be applied locally.
MINERALS: Zinc (preventative).
ESSENTIAL OILS: Tea Tree oil.
TISSUE SALTS: Ferr phos, Kali mur, and Silica.
REFERENCES:
Natural Treatments and Remedies - Global Health
The Complete Natural Health Encyclopedia - David Nyholt.
Health Through God's Pharmacy - M. Treben

CARDIOVASCULAR DISEASE.....

Refer to *Arteriosclerosis* Page 13

CARPAL TUNNEL SYNDROME.....

SINGLE HERBS: Ginger Root Caps.
VITAMINS: B complex, B6, and C.
MINERALS: Calcium and Magnesium.
ESSENTIAL OILS: Birch, Lavender, Marjoram, and Rosemary.
FLOWER REMEDIES: Take Bachs Rescue Remedy.
TISSUE SALTS: Ferr phos, Kali phos, and Mag phos.
ALSO: Bromelain.
REFERENCES:
The Complete Natural Health Encyclopedia - David Nyholt

CAR SICKNESS.....

Refer to *Motion Sickness* Page 49

CATARACTS.....

HERB COMPLEX: The following combinations are available by prescription only. - Cineraria Maritima, D3.
PHYSIOLOGIC ACTION: This product is a Homeopathic medicine and only available through your Homeopathic Doctor. Used regularly, this product will dissolve cataracts completely, after cataracts have disappeared use gencydo for minor inflammation.
HERBAL COMBINATION:
(Herbal Eyebright Formula)
PHYSIOLOGIC ACTION: This herbal product contains valuable nutrients for the eyes. If taken regularly, in conjunction with a proper diet, cataracts are likely to dissolve.
SINGLE HERBS: Standardized Bilberry Extract.
VITAMINS: A, B1, B2, B5, C, and E.

MINERALS: Copper, Manganese, Selenium, and Zinc.
ALSO: L-Lysine neutralizes viruses.
REFERENCES:
The Complete Natural Health Encyclopedia - David Nyholt

CERVICAL CANCER ...
Refer to *Cancer* Page 21

CERVICAL DYSPLASIA
SINGLE HERBS: Bloodroot and Calendula.
VITAMINS: A, B complex, B6, B12, Folic Acid, and C.
MINERALS: Selenium and Zinc.
TISSUE SALTS: Kali mur and Nat sulph.
ALSO: Bitter Orange Oil, Bromelain, and Escarotic treatment.
REFERENCES:
Natural Treatments and Remedies - Global Health

CHARLEY HORSE .....
HERBAL COMBINATIONS: (BF & C)
PHYSIOLOGIC ACTION: This formula aids in the healing process for torn cartilage's, sprained limbs, broken bones, athletic injuries, and associated swelling and inflammation.
SINGLE HERBS: Comfrey, Horsetail, Oat Straw, Skullcap, and Yucca.
VITAMINS: B complex (stress), B1, B2, B5, C, D, and E.
MINERALS: Calcium, Magnesium, and Phosphorous.
ESSENTIAL OILS: Tea Tree Oil.
FLOWER REMEDIES: Use Bachs Rescue Remedy.
TISSUE SALTS: Calc fluor, Ferr phos, Kali mur, and Kali sulph.

ALSO: #12 tissue salts, Green-Lipid Mussel, Silica, Protein, and Unsaturated Fatty Acids.
REFERENCES:
The Athletes Bible – David Nyholt

CHEMICAL ALLERGIES .....
Refer to *Allergies* Page 11

CHICKEN POX .....
HERBAL COMBINATION: (Fenu-Thyme) (ANT-PLG Syrup) (EchinaGuard)
PHYSIOLOGIC ACTION: Helps the body to resist infectious diseases and reduce fever.
SINGLE HERBS: Cayenne, Chickweed, Cleavers, Echinacea, Lobelia, and Red Clover.
ALSO: A bath con be made from bulk chickweed to alleviate itching. Chickweed ointment is also excellent for itching.
VITAMINS: Complete Multivitamin plus A, C, and E.
MINERALS: Multimineral plus Potassium and Zinc.
ESSENTIAL OILS: Lavender.
FLOWER REMEDIES: Hornbeam, Impatiens, and Mustard.
TISSUE SALTS: Ferr phos, Kali mur, and Kali sulph.
REFERENCES:
Communicable Diseases - L. Marks
Herb Manual - E. White

CHRONIC FATIGUE ...
Refer to *Fatigue Chronic* Page 32

CIRCULATION .....
HERBAL COMBINATIONS: (H Formula) (Ginkgold)
PHYSIOLOGIC ACTION: Contains herbs which strengthen the heart and builds the vascular system. When taken with Cayenne, it

improves circulation, giving a warming sensation to the entire body.

ALSO: Cayenne strengthens the pulse rate and circulation while Black Cohosh slows it down.

SINGLE HERBS: Cayenne, Black Cohosh, Bayberry, Butchers Broom, Ginkgo, and Yarrow.

VITAMINS: A, B3, C, E, and Lecithin.

MINERALS: Calcium, Magnesium, and Potassium

ESSENTIAL OILS: Camphor, Cinnamon, Hyssop, and Pine.

FLOWER REMEDIES: Combine Holly, Hornbeam, Impatiens, and Willow.

TISSUE SALTS: Calc phos, Kali sulph, and Nat sulph.

REFERENCES:
Herbally Yours - P. Royal

CIRRHOSIS OF THE LIVER.....

SINGLE HERBS: Barberry, Burdock, Celandine, Dandelion, Echinacea, Fennel, Garlic, Golden Seal, Hops, Milk Thistle, Red Clover, and Suma.

VITAMINS: A, B3, B9, B12, B complex, C, D, E, and K.

MINERALS: Magnesium, and Zinc.

ESSENTIAL OILS: Juniper, Lemon, and Roman Chamomile.

FLOWER REMEDIES: Combine Gorse, Holy, and Impatiens.

TISSUE SALTS: Calc phos, Kali phos, Nat mur, and Silicea.

ALSO: Carbohydrates, Coenzyme Q10, L-Carnitine, L-Glutathionine, L-Methionine, and Protein.

REFERENCES:
The Complete Natural Health Encyclopedia - David Nyholt

Natural Treatments and Remedies - Global Health

CLAP.....
Refer to *Gonorrhea* Page 36

CLUSTER HEADACHES.....
Refer to *Migraines* Page 48

COLD FEET.....
HERBAL COMBINATION:
(Cayenne extract)
PHYSIOLOGIC ACTION:
Improves pulse rate and circulation giving a warming sensation to the entire body.
SINGLE HERBS: Cayenne, Bayberry, and Kelp.
VITAMINS: Vitamin E and Niacin.
MINERALS: A complete multimineral complex.
TISSUE SALTS: Kali sulph.
REFERENCES:
Herbally Yours - P. Royal
Vitamin Bible - E. Mindell

COLDS AND COUGHS..
HERBAL COMBINATIONS:
(Fenu-Thyme) (Garlic Syrup)
(Loquat Syrup) (Garlicin CF)
PHYSIOLOGIC ACTION: These herbal syrups and combinations work to soothe the throat and lungs and act as expectorants and demulcents to cut and expel mucus from the lungs. Garlicin CF is a unique formula combining the natural benefits of Garlic with other herbs such as Echinacea, Vitamin C, bioflavanoids and Zinc.

COLDS AND FLU.....
HERBAL COMBINATIONS: (C+F)
(Herbal Influence) (ANT-PLG Syrup)

PHYSIOLOGIC ACTION: Proven herbal formulas to help relieve symptoms of colds, flu, hoarseness, colic, cramps, sluggish circulation, beginning of fevers and germinal viral infections. Herbal Influence (formerly known as Herbal Composition) this formula was created by the early American herbalist, Samuel Thomson. It contains herbs which help with fever and nausea.

SINGLE HERBS: Cayenne, Red Clover, Raspberry Tea, Chaparral, Rose Hips, Garlic, Honey, and Golden Seal.

VITAMINS: A, B6, C, and P.

MINERALS: A Multi-mineral complex.

ESSENTIAL OILS: Use Basil, Eucalyptus, Peppermint, and Pine.

FLOWER REMEDIES: Impatiens.

TISSUE SALTS: Ferr phos, Kali mur, and Nat Mur.

REFERENCES:
How to Get Well - P. Airola

COLD SORES .....
(Herpes Simplex)

VITAMINS: Vitamin C with Vitamin P, and vitamin E oil applied directly.

MINERALS: Zinc.

ESSENTIAL OILS: Lavender, Lemon, and Thyme.

TISSUE SALTS: Kali phos.

ALSO: Lysine, and Primodophilus.

REFERENCES:
Vitamin Bible - E. Mindell

COLIC (BABIES) .....

HERBAL COMBINATION:
(Catnip and Fennel Extract)

PHYSIOLOGIC ACTION: This formula works on minor spasms, acid stomach and gas. It also soothes indigestion and nerves. Excellent for children.

SINGLE HERBS: Catnip, Fennel, Camomile, Peppermint or any combination in a tea. Make teas very mild. No sugar. Check your own diet if nursing baby.

FLOWER REMEDIES: Take Bachs Rescue Remedy.

TISSUE SALTS: Mag phos.

REFERENCES:
The Complete Natural Health Encyclopedia - David Nyholt.
Herbally Yours - P. Royal

COLITIS .....

SPECIFICS: Mucous Colitis is often associated with, and made worse by psychological stress. Emotional upset should be avoided. Various herbs with multiple properties must be used to address the complexity of this situation.

Single herbs to be used in combination: Bayberry, Camomile, Garlic, Reshi Mushroom, Valerian, and Wild Yam.

ALSO: Avoid citrus juices. Bananas are very soothing and healing in ulcerative colitis. Primadophilus is effective in stabilizing flora in lower bowel.

SINGLE HERBS: Alfalfa, Bayberry, Camomile, Caraway, Garlic, Peppermint, Reshi Mushroom, Plantain, Valerian, and Wild Yam.

VITAMINS: A, B6, B Complex, C, and E.

MINERALS: Calcium Lactate, Iron, Magnesiun, and Potassium.

ESSENTIAL OILS: Ylang-Ylang.

FLOWER REMEDIES: Combine Holy, Hornbeam, and Impatiens.

REFERENCES:
How to Get Well - P. Airola
The Complete Natural Health Encyclopedia - David Nyholt.
Indian Herbology of North America - A. Hutchens

COLORECTAL CANCER

Refer to *Cancer* Page 21

COMMON MEASLES...

Refer to *Measles* Page 47

CONFUSION.....

Refer to *Memory Loss* Page 47

CONSTIPATION.....

HERBAL COMBINATIONS: (Multilax #2) or (Naturalax #2) (Laxacil) (Naturalax 1) (Naturalax 3) (Aloelax Formula)

PHYSIOLOGIC ACTION: There are two forms of laxatives, stimulant and bulk forming. Stimulant laxatives encourage peristalsis of the bowel. This motion empties the intestinal tract of waste. Bulk forming laxatives absorb water and toxic wastes from the intestinal walls. The natural expansion triggers peristalsis, and pushes old fecal matter through the bowel. Both forms of laxatives have benefits.

Warning: Most laxatives should not be taken during pregnancy. Psyllium husks, however, are safe.

SINGLE HERBS: Aloe Vera, Cascara Sagrada, Psyllium, and Senna.

Babies: Licorice tea (made weakly). Nursing mothers can pass this one to the infant.

VITAMINS: A, B Complex, C, D. and E.

MINERALS: Calcium, Magnesiun, Potassium, and Zinc.

ESSENTIAL OILS: Basil, Fennel, Lavender, and Rose.

TISSUE SALTS: Silicea.

ALSO: Primadophilus

REFERENCES:
Herbally Yours - P. Royal
Vitamin Bible - E. Mindell
How to Get Well - P. Airola

COUGHS.....

HERBAL TONICS: Pie Pa Koa, Salus, Olbas, and Swiss herbal candy.

VITAMINS: A, B6, C, and P.

MINERALS: Zinc.

ESSENTIAL OILS: Basil and Pine.

FLOWER REMEDIES: Impatiens.

TISSUE SALTS: Ferr phos, Kali mur, and Nat mur.

ALSO: Fenugreek Seed, Comfrey Leaves, Garlic, Honey, Rose Hips, fresh juice, short fasts, and Zinc Lozenges.

REFERENCES:
The Miracle of Garlic - P.Airola
Health Through God's Pharmacy - M. Treben

CRADLE CAP.....

PHYSIOLOGICAL ACTION: Olive oil or vitamin E on the head and brush gently.

ESSENTIAL OILS: Lavender.

FLOWER REMEDIES: Rock Rose.

TISSUE SALTS: Kali sulph and Nat phos.

ALSO: A mild dandruff shampoo can be used.

REFERENCES:
Herbally Yours - P. Royal
The Complete Natural Health Encyclopedia - David Nyholt.

CRAMPS.....

Refer to *Leg Cramps* or *Menstrual Cramps* in Guide

CROHN'S DISEASE....

SINGLE HERBS: Echinacea, Garlic, Golden Seal, Pau d'Arco, Rose Hips, and Yerba Mate.

VITAMINS: A, B12, B complex, and E.

MINERALS: A Complete Mineral Complex.

FLOWER REMEDIES: Hornbeam, Mimulus, and Mustard.
TISSUE SALTS: Kali mur, Kali phos, Mag phos, and Nat sulph.
ALSO: Acidophlus, Aloe Vera, Essential fatty acids, and Protein.
REFERENCES:
Complete Natural Health Encyclopedia - David Nyholt
Natural Treatments and Remedies - Global Health

CROUP . . . . .
HERBAL COMBINATIONS:
(Breath aid) (BRE)
PHYSIOLOGIC ACTION: Helps to restore free breathing by opening up the bronchial passages. Effective for shortness of breath, tightness of chest, and wheezing associated with croup.
SINGLE HERBS: Comfrey, Echinacea tincture, Fenugreek, and Golden Seal.
VITAMINS: A, C, and E.
MINERALS: Zinc.
ESSENTIAL OILS: Chamomile, Eucalyptus, Lavender, and Thyme.
FLOWER REMEDIES: Take Bachs Rescue Remedy.
TISSUE SALTS: Kali sulph and Nat sulph.
ALSO: Cod Liver Oil and Protein.
REFERENCES:
Herbally Yours - P. Royal
The Complete Natural Health Encyclopedia - David Nyholt

CYSTITIS . . . . .
Refer to *Kidney & Bladder* P 43

DANDRUFF . . . . .
SINGLE HERBS: Burdock, Chaparral, Red Clover, and Yarrow, (used as teas or rubbed on the head).
VITAMINS: A, B complex, B6, C, and E.

MINERALS: Selenium and Zinc.
ESSENTIAL OILS: Tea Tree Oil.
FLOWER REMEDIES: Combine Red Chestnut and White Chestnut.
TISSUE SALTS: Kali sulph and Nat mur.
ALSO: Unsaturated fatty acids.
REFERENCES:
Back to Eden - J. Kloss
Stop Hair Loss - P. Airola

DEAFNESS . . . . .
Refer to *Ear Infection* Page 30

DEPRESSION . . . . .
HERBAL COMBINATIONS:
(Ginseng, Gotu Kola Plus) (Adren-Aid)
PHYSIOLOGIC ACTION: These excellent formulas build zest, energy, stamina, mental alertness and reflex action. The herbs also help provide adrenal support which affect depression.
SINGLE HERBS: Bee Pollen, Cayenne, Damiana, Gotu Kola, St. John's Wort, Skullcap, Shitaki Mushroom, Siberian Ginseng, and Yucca.
VITAMINS: B3, B6, B12, B complex (stress), and lots of Vit C.
MINERALS: Multi-mineral Complex plus Calcium, Chromium, Magnesium, and Zinc.
ESSENTIAL OILS: .Neroli, Rose, and Ylang-Ylang.
FLOWER REMEDIES: Take Bachs Rescue Remedy.
TISSUE SALTS: Kali phos, Nat mur, and Nat Sulph.
ALSO: Tryptophan and L-Tyrosine
REFERENCES:
Every Woman's Book - P. Airola
Amino Acids Book - C. Wade
Drugs and Beyond - David Nyholt
Fighting Depression - Ross
The Athletes Bible - David Nyholt

DERMATITIS.....

HERBAL COMBINATION: (AKN)
PHYSIOLOGIC ACTION: Many skin problems are related to liver dysfunction. This formula gives support to the liver, helps to cleanse the blood, and supplies nutrients for the skin.
SINGLE HERBS: Aloe Vera (on skin), Burdock, Cleavers, Dandelion, Evening Primrose, Garlic, Golden Seal, Pau d'Arco, and Yellowdock.
VITAMINS: A, B complex, B2, B3, B6, D, E, and Biotin B Complex.
MINERALS: Sulfur ointment, Zinc, and Potassium.
ESSENTIAL OILS: Geranium, Lavender, Myrrh, Neroli, and Rose.
FLOWER REMEDIES: Chickory, Crabapple, Holly, and Impatiens.
TISSUE SALTS: Kali sulph and Nat phos.
ALSO: Yu-ccan herbal drink.
REFERENCES:
Nutrition Almanac - J. Kirshmann

DIABETES.....

HERBAL COMBINATION: (PC)
PHYSIOLOGIC ACTION: An excellent formula to stimulate and restore natural functions, of the pancreas and spleen. Contains a natural form of insulin thus relieving most symptoms associated with diabetes.
SINGLE HERBS: Cayenne, Cedar Berries, Licorice Root, Mullein, Suma, Juniper and Uva Ursi.
VITAMINS: A, B complex, B1, B2, B6, B12, C, E, P, Choline, and Inositol.
MINERALS: Calcium, Chromium, Iron, Potassium, Magnesium, and Zinc.
ESSENTIAL OILS: Cedar, Eucalyptus, Geranium, and Juniper.

FLOWER REMEDIES: Gentain, Gorse, and Sweet Chestnut.
ALSO: Protein and Proteolytic Enzymes.
REFERENCES:
How to Get Well - P. Airola

DIAPER RASH.....

HERBAL OINTMENTS: (X-Itch ointment) (Derm-Aid Ointment)
SINGLE HERBS: Mullein Leaf, and Slippery Elm (used internally in juice or apply as paste).
ALSO: Vitamin E, Powdered Golden Seal, or Comfrey added to baby powder.
VITAMINS: Mom can take Vitamins A, B, and C.
ESSENTIAL OILS: Tea Tree Oil.
FLOWER REMEDIES: Use Rescue Remedy cream.
TISSUE SALTS: Silicea.
REFERENCES:
Herbally Yours - P. Royal
The Complete Natural Health Encyclopedia - David Nyholt.

DIARRHEA.....

HERBAL COMBINATION: (Diarid)
PHYSIOLOGICAL ACTION: This is a maximum-strength formula that relieves diarrhea and the pain and cramping that accompany it. The active ingredient is called Activated Attapulgite, a special kaolin substance with water absorbing abilities.
SINGLE HERBS: Blackberry Root, Red Raspberry, Slippery Elm, and Yucca.
ALSO: Nutmeg and Cloves for cramps.
VITAMINS: A, B complex, B1, B2, B3, B6, C, Folic Acid, and Choline.

MINERALS: Calcium, Chlorine, Iron, Magnesium, Potassium, and Sodium.
ESSENTIAL OILS: Chamomile, Lavender, and Peppermint.
FLOWER REMEDIES: Mimulus.
TISSUE SALTS: Ferr phos and Nat sulph.
ALSO: Acidophilus, and Activated Charcoal.
Babies and Children: Slippery Elm enema, Red Raspberry tea, fresh apple juice, banana, carob.
REFERENCES:
How to Get Well - P. Airola

DIGESTIVE DISORDER

HERBAL COMBINATIONS:
(Multilax #2) or (Naturalax #2)
PHYSIOLOGIC ACTION: Helps intestinal gas, indigestion, heart-burn, and stomach ache. Warm Peppermint tea, Cayenne, Papaya, or Aloe Vera can be taken with meals.
SINGLE HERBS: Aloe Vera, Chamomile, Cayenne, Comfrey leaves, Fennel, Ginger, Golden Seal, Licorice, Marshmallow Root, and Papaya.
VITAMINS: A, B3, B complex, and Biotin.
MINERALS: Copper, Dolomite, Iodine, Phosphorus, Potassium, and Zinc.
ESSENTIAL OILS: Bergamot, Dill, Lavender, and Ylang-Ylang.
FLOWER REMEDIES: Combine Holly, Hornbean, and Impatiens.
TISSUE SALTS: Calc phos, Kali mur, and Mag phos.
ALSO: Digestive Enzymes, Garlic, Bee Pollen, Calmus Root tea, Lactic Acid foods, Sweetish Bitters, Primodophlus and Yu-ccan herbal drink.
REFERENCES:
Herbally Yours - P. Royal

Digestive Enzymes - R.Passwater

DIZZINESS . . . . .
Refer to *Vertigo* Page 65

DROPSY . . . . .

HERBAL COMBINATIONS: (KB)
PHYSIOLOGIC ACTION: KB acts as a mild diuretic to rid the body of excessive water.
SINGLE HERBS: Alfalfa, Buchu, Dandelion, tea, Juniper, Lobelia, Pau d' Arco tea, Safflower, Uva Ursi, and Yarrow.
VITAMINS: B1, B6, B complex, C, D, and E.
MINERALS: Calcium, Copper, and Potassium.
ESSENTIAL OILS: Grapefruit and Rosemary.
FLOWER REMEDIES: Chicory and Mimulus.
TISSUE SALTS: Nat sulph.
ALSO: L-Taurine, #9 and #11 Tissue Salts, Silicon, and Protein.
REFERENCES:
The Complete Natural Health Encyclopedia - David Nyholt
Natural Treatments and Remedies - Global Health
Nutrition Almanac - J. Kirshmann

DRUG DEPENDENCY . .

HERBAL COMBINATIONS:
(Adren Aid) and (Red Clover Comb)
PHYSIOLOGIC ACTION: These herbal formulas provide support to the body while cleansing toxins. Red Clover Combination should be used with all detoxification programs.
SINGLE HERBS: Pau d'Arco, Camomile tea, Licorice Root, and Lobelia.
VITAMINS: B complex, and C.
MINERALS: Calcium, and Potassium.

ESSENTIAL OILS: Geranium, Lavender, Lemon, and Chamomile.

FLOWER REMEDIES: Combine Holly, Impatiens, Larch, Rock Water, Olive, and Chestnut.

TISSUE SALTS: Calc phos and Nat mur.

ALSO: Tyrosine, Vitamins B, C, and E, alleviate depression, fatigue and irritability when dependent on cocaine, hashish, and marijuana. Refer to: "Note in SMOKING" in this manual.

REFERENCES:
Drugs and Beyond - David Nyholt
The Athletes Bible - David Nyholt

DYSPEPSIA .....
Refer *Digestive Disorders* **P 29**

EAR INFECTIONS .....

HERBAL COMBINATIONS: (Immun Aid) (B&B Extract) and (EchinaGuard)

PHYSIOLOGIC ACTION:
ImmunAid boosts immunity, thereby helping with ear infections. EchinaGuard is a liquid. Echinacea extract is excellent for small children with ear infections. B&B Extract can be placed in the ear or taken internally. It is also used to aid poor equilibrium, and nervous conditions.

SINGLE HERBS: Blue Cohosh, Echinacea, Garlic Oil, Garlic, Mullein Oil, Mullein, Skullcap, and St. Johns Wort.

VITAMINS: A, B complex, and C.

MINERALS: Calcium and Zinc.

ESSENTIAL OILS: Marjoram, Rosemary, and Tea Tree oil.

FLOWER REMEDIES: Take Bachs Rescue Remedy.

TISSUE SALTS: Ferr phos, Kali phos, and Silicea.

ALSO: Propolis, and Primadophilus. When combating ear infections, it is imperative to exclude allergen foods from the diet. This is particularly true of all dairy products.

REFERENCES:
The Complete Natural Health Encyclopedia - David Nyholt.
Back to Eden - J. Kloss

ECZEMA .....

HERBAL COMBINATION: (AKN)
PHYSIOLOGIC ACTION: When toxins are not properly eliminated from the body, they may surface through the skin creating eczema. This formula has been created to support liver and gall bladder function, to ensure toxins are filtered from the blood.

SINGLE HERBS: Aloe Vera, Chickweed, Evening Primrose Oil, Pau d'Arco, Red Clover, Thisilyn (Milk Thistle), and Yellow Dock.

VITAMINS: A, B complex, C, D, Paba, Biotin, Choline, and Inositol.

MINERALS: Magnesium, Sulfur Ointment, and Zinc Ointment.

ESSENTIAL OILS: Elemi, Myrrh, Neroli, and Rose.

FLOWER REMEDIES: Use Rescue Remedy cream.

TISSUE SALTS: Ferr phos, Kali mur Kali sulph, and Nat mur.

ALSO: This condition is aggravated by food allergens such as dairy and wheat. These foods should be avoided. Powders and pastes should not be applied during acute or weeping stages. After acute stage passes, ointments and salves may be applied. Herbal ointments which contain Chickweed and Calendula are particularly helpful.

REFERENCES:
How to Get Well - P. Airola

EDEMA .....

HERBAL COMBINATION: (KB)

PHYSIOLOGIC ACTION: KB acts as a mild diuretic to rid the body of excessive water.
SINGLE HERBS: Buchu, Dandelion tea, Juniper, Parsley, Safflower, Uva Ursi, and Yarrow.
VITAMINS: B1, B6, B complex, C, D, and E.
MINERALS: Calcium, Copper, and Potassium.
ESSENTIAL OILS: Grapefruit.
FLOWER REMEDIES: Chicory and Mimulus.
TISSUE SALTS: Nat sulph.
ALSO: #9, #11 tissue salts, Protein, and low sodium.

EJACULATION INVOLUNTARY.....
Refer to *Impotence* Page 42

EMPHYSEMA.....
HERBAL COMBINATIONS: (Breath-Aid) (BronCare) (Garlicin CF)
PHYSIOLOGICAL ACTION: These natural formulas help to restore free breathing by dilating bronchial passages. They also offer nutritional support to the lungs.
SINGLE HERBS: Anise Seed Oil, Comfrey, Elecampane, Garlic, Lobelia, Mullein, and Swedish Bitters.
VITAMINS: A, B complex, C, D, E, Folic Acid.
ESSENTIAL OILS: Tea Tree Oil.
FLOWER REMEDIES: Combine Holly, Hornbean, Impatiens, and Mimulus.
TISSUE SALTS: Kali phos, Mag phos, and Nat mur.
ALSO: L-Cysteine, and L-Methionine,
REFERENCES:
Stop Hair Loss - P. Airola
How to Get Well - P. Airola

ENDOMETRIAL CANCER.....
Refer to *Cancer* Page 21

ENTEROBIASIS.....
Refer to *Parasites* Page 53

EPILEPSY.....
HERBAL COMBINATION: (B&B Tincture)
PHYSIOLOGICAL ACTION: The herbs in this formula have a beneficial effect on the autonomic nervous system. It helps to calm the nerves and relax the muscles.
ALSO: Avoid all refined sugars, completely eliminate all animal proteins, except milk as they rob body of magnesium and Vitamin B6 reserves. Eat lots of raw vegetables and fruit. Epileptics require plenty of fresh air, exercise and sound sleep.
SINGLE HERBS: Black-Cohosh, Horse Nettle, Hyssop, Irish Moss, Mistletoe, and Skullcap.
VITAMINS: A, B complex, Niacin, B6, B15, C, D, and E.
MINERALS: Calcium, Chromium, Iron, and Magnesium.
ESSENTIAL OILS: Basil, Lavender, and Rosemary.
FLOWER REMEDIES: Take Bachs Rescue Remedy.
TISSUE SALTS: Ferr phos and Kali phos.
ALSO: Germanium, L-Taurine, L-Tyrosine, Proteolytic Enzymes, and Digestive Enzymes.
REFERENCES:
Body Mind and Sugar - E. Pezel
The Complete Natural Health Encyclopedia - David Nyholt.
Convulsive Disorders - H. Keith
How to Get Well - P. Airola

EPSTEIN BARR VIRUS . . . . .
Refer to *Fatigue Chronic* P 32

ERECTION PROBLEMS . . . . .
Refer to *Impotence* Page 42

EYE DISORDERS . . . . .
HERBAL COMBINATION:
(Herbal Eyebright Formula)
PHYSIOLOGIC ACTION: Extremely valuable in strengthening and healing the eyes. Aids the body in healing lesions and eye injuries.
Warning: If symptoms persist, discontinue use.
ALSO: The herb eyebright may be used as a wash for superficial inflammations of the eye.
SINGLE HERBS: Bilberry, and Eyebright.
VITAMINS: A, B1, B2, B3, B5, B6, C D, and E.
MINERALS: Calcium, Copper, Mangan- ese, Selenium, Magnesium and Zinc.
TISSUE SALTS: Ferr phos, Kali Phos, and Nat Mur.
ALSO: Gyncydo and Protein.
REFERENCES:
Herbally Yours - P. Royal
Vision Revised - Donsbach

FATIGUE - STRESS (Chronic) . . . . .
HERBAL COMBINATIONS:
(Adren Aid) (Echinacea Astragalus and Reshi Combination) (ImmuneAid) (Healthy Greens)
PHYSIOLOGIC ACTION: The herbs in these combinations work to support the adrenal glands and act as a tonic boost to the immune system.

ALSO: Recent studies have shown that a combination of Evening Primrose Oil, and Fish Oil is very beneficial in combating chronic fatigue. The original study used a product called, "Efamol Marine." This product is not available in the United States nor Canada. It can be replicated by combining the individual Evening Primrose Oil capsules with Fish Oil, or Fish Liver Oil.
SINGLE HERBS: Astragalus, Cayenne, Echinacea, Siberian Ginseng, Ginseng, Gota Kola, Lobelia, Reshi Mushroom, and all deep green herbs such as Barley Grass, Chlorella, Spirulina, and Garlic.
VITAMINS: A, Ester C with Bioflavonoids, B complex (high potency), E, D, and Folic Acid.
MINERALS: Iron, Magnesium, Manganese, Potassium, Selenium, and Zinc.
ESSENTIAL OILS: Chamomile, Lavender, Pine and Spearmint.
FLOWER REMEDIES: Take Bachs Rescue Remedy and White Chestnut.
TISSUE SALTS: Ferr phos, Kali phos, and Silicea.
ALSO: Canaid and Yu-ccan herbal drinks, Coenzyme Q 10, and Raw Thymus.
REFERENCES:
Herbally Yours - P. Royal
Ginseng - Donsbach

FATIGUE (CHRONIC)
HERBAL COMBINATIONS:
Recent studies have shown that a combination of Evening Primrose Oil, and Fish Oil is very beneficial in combating chronic fatigue. The original study called, "Efamol Marine." This product is not available in the United States nor Canada. It can be replicated by

combining the individual Evening Primrose Oil capsules with Fish Oil, or Fish Liver Oil.

Other combinations include: AdrenAid, Echinacea Astragalus and Reshi Combination, ImmuneAid, & Healthy Greens.

PHYSIOLOGICAL ACTION: The herbs in these combinations work to support the adrenal glands and acts as a tonic boost to the immune system.

SINGLE HERBS: Astragalus, Echinacea, EchinaGuard Liquid Extract, Siberian Ginseng, Reshi Mushroom, all deep green herbs such as Barley Grass, Chlorella, Spirulina, and Garlic.

VITAMINS: Ester C with Bioflavonoids, B Complex, E, and D.

MINERALS: Calcium, Magnesium, Potassium, Selenium, and Zinc.

ESSENTIAL OILS: Lavender, Rose, and Rosemary.

FLOWER REMEDIES: Olive.

TISSUE SALTS: Silicea.

ALSO: CoQ 10, and Raw Thymus.

REFERENCES:
The Athletes Bible – David Nyholt
The Fitness Formula - S. Sokol

FATIGUE (GENERAL)

HERBAL COMBINATION:
(Herbal UP) (Energizer) (AdrenAid)

PHYSIOLOGIC ACTION: These herbal formulas combine herbs which support the adrenals, tone the system, and offer stamina, and improve performance.

SINGLE HERBS: Siberian Ginseng, Gotu Kola, and Bee Pollen.

VITAMINS: Multivitamin, plus B Complex, B 12, and Vitamin C.

MINERALS: GTF Chromium, Potassium, Selenium, and Zinc.

ESSENTIAL OILS:. Grapefruit, Lavender, Neroli, and Niaouli.

TISSUE SALTS: Ferr phos.
REFERENCES:
The Athletes Bible – David Nyholt
The Fitness Formula - S. Sokol

FEVER - FLU .....

HERBAL COMBINATIONS:
(Fenu-Thyme) (Herbal Influence) and (Immune Aid).

PHYSIOLOGIC ACTION: These effective formulas help to cleanse toxins, combat infections and inflammations especially in the lymphatic system. They give support to the immune system enabling the body to combat the illness.

VITAMINS: A, B complex, B3, C, E, and P.

MINERALS: Calcium, Phosphorus, Potassium, and Sodium.

ESSENTIAL OILS: Basil, Eucalyptus, Peppermint, and Pine.

FLOWER REMEDIES: Impatiens.

TISSUE SALTS: Ferr phos, Kali phos, and Kali sulph.

ALSO: Canaid herbal drink, Propolis, Red Raspberry, Elder Flowers, Garlic, Rosehip, Golden Seal, Yarrow, Red Clover, #4 tissue salts.

Catnip and Peppermint together at onset of flu. Lemon or Grapefruit juice.

Babies and Children: Red Raspberry or Peppermint tea.

REFERENCES:
The incurables - Christopher
Herbally Yours - P. Royal

FIBROIDS .....
Refer to *Tumors Benign* Page 64

FLATULENCE .....
Refer to *Digestive Disorders* Page 29

FLUID RETENTION ...
Refer *Dropsy* Page 29

FOOD POISONING .....
SINGLE HERBS: Cat Claw, Golden Seal, and Pau d' Arco.
VITAMINS: C and E.
MINERALS: Multi mineral complex.
ESSENTIAL OILS: Garlic, Pepper, and Thyme.
FLOWER REMEDIES: Take Bachs Rescue Remedy.
TISSUE SALTS: Kali phos, Nat mur, and Nat phos.
ALSO: Acidophlus, L-Cysteine, L-Methionine, and Fiber.
REFERENCES:
The Complete Natural Health Encyclopedia - David Nyholt

FRACTURE .....
HERBAL COMBINATION: (BF+C).
PHYSIOLOGIC ACTION: This formula aids the healing processes involved with broken bones and athletic injuries.
SINGLE HERBS: Comfrey Root, Black Walnut, Horsetail, Lobelia, Skullcap, and White Oak Bark.
VITAMINS: A, C, and D.
MINERALS: Calcium, Magnesium, and Potassium.
ESSENTIAL OILS: Bergamot, Birch, Geranium, and Rosemary.
FLOWER REMEDIES: Take Bachs Rescue Remedy.
ALSO: Silicon and Protein.
REFERENCES:
The Athletes Bible – David Nyholt
The Fitness Formula - S. Sokol

FRIGIDITY .....
HERBAL COMBINATIONS: (APH)

PHYSIOLOGIC ACTION:
Stimulates male and female sexual impulses as well as strengthens and increases sexual power and helps fight fatigue.
SINGLE HERBS: Damiana, Gingko, Ginseng, and Goto Kola.
VITAMINS: E, Paba, Folic Acid, and Lecithin.
MINERALS: Calcium, Iodine, and Zinc.
TISSUE SALTS: Calc phos.
ALSO: L-Arginine, L-Tyrosine, Proteolytic Enzymes, Melbrosia (for men), Bee Pollen, and Sesame Seeds.
REFERENCES:
The Complete Natural Health Encyclopedia - David Nyholt
Natural Treatments and Remedies - Global Health

FUNGUS INFESTATIONS .....
(Athletes foot and Thrush)
VITAMINS: A, B, C, and E.
ESSENTIAL OILS: Tea Tree Oil.
TISSUE SALTS: Silicea.
ALSO: Primadophilus, Black Walnut, and Caprinex.
REFERENCES:
Back to Eden - J. Kloss

GAS INTESTINAL .....
HERBAL COMBINATION: (LG)
PHYSIOLOGIC ACTION: Excellent formula for relieving intestinal gas, also cleanses liver and gall bladder.
SINGLE HERBS: Catnip, Ginger, Peppermint, and Horseradish are helpful for colon gas.
VITAMINS: B complex, B1, and B5.
TISSUE SALTS: Mag phos, Nat phos, and Nat sulph.

ALSO: Eucarbon, Primadophilus, #8 tissue salts, and activated charcoal.
REFERENCES:
How to Get Well - P. Airola

GASTRITIS .....

SINGLE HERBS: Calamus, Chamomile, Dandelion, Marshmallow, Meadowsweet, and Swedish Bitters.
VITAMINS: A, B complex, B6, B12, C, D, E, and Lecithin.
MINERALS: Calcium and Iron.
ESSENTIAL OILS: Orange and Lavender.
FLOWER REMEDIES: Combine Holly, Impatiens, and White Chestnut.
TISSUE SALTS: Calc phos, Nat phos, and Mag Phos.
ALSO: Diet and lifestyle influence this condition. It is important to avoid all food irritants such as spices and fiber. Avoid acidic foods such as tomatoes and citrus fruits. Stress reduction is important.
REFERENCES:
Herbally Yours - P. Royal

GERMAN MEASLES
Refer to *Measles* Page 47

GINGERVITIS .....

SINGLE HERBS: Chamomile, Echinacea, Lobelia, Myrrh Gum, and White Oak Bark.
VITAMINS: A, B complex, C, D, P, Niacin, and Folic Acid.
MINERALS: Calcium, Copper, Magnesium, Manganese, Phosphorus, Potassium, Silicon, Sodium, and Zinc.
ESSENTIAL OILS: Myrrh, Tea Tree, and Thyme
TISSUE SALTS: Ferr phos and Kali phos.

ALSO: Coenzyme Q10, Protein, and Unsaturated Fats.
REFERENCES:
The Complete Natural Health Encyclopedia - David Nyholt
Natural Treatments and Remedies - Global Health

GLAND INFECTIONS ...

HERBAL COMBINATION: (IGL)
PHYSIOLOGIC ACTION: Combats infection and reduces inflammation from the body, especially the lymphatic system, ears, throat, lungs, breasts and organs of the body.
VITAMINS: C
ESSENTIAL OILS: Tea Tree Oil.
TISSUE SALTS: Ferr phos and Kali phos.
ALSO: Propolis, Golden Seal, Saw Palmetto, and Echinacea.
REFERENCES:
Glandular Extracts - Donsbach
Herbally Yours - P. Royal
Health Through God's Pharmacy - M. Treben

GLAND PROBLEMS ...

HERBAL COMBINATIONS: (GL) (IF)
PHYSIOLOGIC ACTION:
Effective for swollen lymph nodes and in helping the body fight glandular weakness and infections.
SINGLE HERBS: Alfalfa, Calendula, Echinacea, Golden Seal, Lobelia, Mullein, Saw Palmetto, and Skullcap.
VITAMINS: A, B5, B Complex, C, and E.
MINERALS: Calcium, Magnesium, and Potassium.
ALSO: Multi-Glandulars, Primrose Oil.
REFERENCES:
Glandular Extracts - Donsbach
Herbally Yours - P. Royal

GLAUCOMA .....

(Hypertension of the eye)

SPECIFICS: It is believed that restoration of vision lost due to nerve degeneration cannot occur. However the vitamins and herbs listed can be effective in controlling and preserving the remaining sight.

HERBAL SUPPLEMENTATION: Herbal Eyebright Formula, KB, Bilberry, and Extress.

PHYSIOLOGIC ACTION: These herbs work to restore balance to the system. They supply nutrition to the eye, while helping to remove excessive fluids and toxins. They also help to reduce problems associated with stress.

NOTE: It is important to keep in contact with your doctor while working with this serious eye problem.

HERB COMBINATION: (Eyebright Comb)

VITAMINS: A, B2, B5, B Complex, C, D, and E.

MINERALS: A good comprehensive muti- mineral formula.

ESSENTIAL OILS: Clary Sage, Lavender, and Rose.

FLOWER REMEDIES: Mustard and Vervain.

ALSO: Germanium.

REFERENCES:
How to Get Well - P. Airola
Health Bulletin - Feb 15, 1964

GOITER .....

SINGLE HERBS: Kelp is an excellent source of iodine.

VITAMINS: A, B6, B complex Choline, C, and E..

MINERALS: Calcium and Iodine.

ESSENTIAL OILS: Lavender and Rosemary.

FLOWER REMEDIES: Combine Holly, Impatiens, and White Chestnut.

TISSUE SALTS: Kali phos.

ALSO: Protein.

REFERENCES:
Natural Treatments and Remedies

GONORRHEA .....

SINGLE HERBS: Echinacea, Golden Seal, Pau d' Arco, and Suma.

VITAMINS: B complex and K.

MINERALS: Zinc.

ESSENTIAL OILS: Neroli and Niaouli.

FLOWER REMEDIES: Combine Holly, Hornbean, Impatiens, and White Chestnut.

TISSUE SALTS: Ferr phos, Kali phos, and Nat mur.

ALSO: Acidophilus, Coenzyme Q10, Germanium, and Protein.

REFERENCES:
Complete Natural Health Encyclopedia - David Nyholt

GOUT .....

HERBAL COMBINATION: (Yucca AR), (Rheum Aid) (Yu-ccan herbal drink)

PHYSIOLOGIC ACTION: These formulas are effective in helping to reduce swelling and inflammation in body joints and connective tissues. Also helps relieve stiffness and pain.

SINGLE HERBS: Burdock, Dandelion Root, Lobelia, Stinging Nettle, Safflower, Pau d'Arco tea, and Yucca.

VITAMINS: A, B complex, B5, C, and E.

MINERALS: Calcium, Magnesium, and Potassium.

ESSENTIAL OILS: Eucalyptus, Juniper, and Rosemary.

FLOWER REMEDIES: Combine Beech, Holy, and Vervain.

ALSO: Primadophilus. Diet plays a vital function in the treatment of this malady. Foods containing Uric Acids, such as meat, and rich pastries need to be avoided. All purine-rich foods need to be avoided, such as anchovies, herring, sardines, mushrooms, mussels, and liver.

REFERENCES:
The Athletes Bible – David Nyholt
The Fitness Formula - S. Sokol

GRIPPE.....
Refer to *Colds and Flu* **Page 24**

GROWTH PROBLEMS..
Refer to *Thyroid* **Page 63**

GYNECOLOGICAL PROBLEMS.....

HERBAL COMBINATION: (Fem-Mend)

PHYSIOLOGIC ACTION: Menstrual regulator, tonic for genito-urinary system. Helpful for severe menstrual discomforts. Acts as an aid in rebuilding a malfunctioning reproductive system (Uterus, ovaries, fallopian tubes)

SINGLE HERBS: Aloe Vera, Blessed Thistle, Comfrey Root, Garlic, Ginger, Golden Seal Root, Red Raspberry, Slippery Elm Bark, Uva Ursi, and Yellow Dock Root,

VITAMINS: A, B Complex, C, E.

MINERALS: Multi-mineral.

ESSENTIAL OILS: Cypress, Fennel, Geranium, and Juniper.

FLOWER REMEDIES: Combine Holly, Impatiens, Olive, and Rock Water.

TISSUE SALTS: Calc phos and Kali sulph.

REFERENCES:
Fitness Formula - Steve Sokol

HANGOVER.....
VITAMINS: A, B complex, B1, B2, B6, B12, C, D, E, and K.

MINERALS: Calcium, Chromium, Iron, Magnesium, Manganese, Selenium, and Zinc.

HARDENING OF THE ARTERIES.....
Refer to *Arteriosclerosis* **Page13**

HAY FEVER.....
HERBAL COMBINATIONS: (HAS Original and Fast Acting Formulas) (Allergy Care)

PHYSIOLOGIC ACTION: These herbal formulas contain a natural extract of Pseudoepheda, in a base of herbs, which help to restore free breathing without causing drowsiness. HAS original is for those sensitive to Ephedra.

SINGLE HERBS: EchinaGuard Nettle tea, Elder Flowers, Eye Bright, Golden Seal, Golden Rod, Swedish Bitters, and Yarrow

VITAMINS: A, B complex, B6, Ester C with Bioflavaniods, and E.

ESSENTIAL OILS: Basil, Peppermint, and Pine.

FLOWER REMEDIES: Chicory, Gentain, Impatiens, and Larch.

TISSUE SALTS: Fer phos, Kali phos, and Nat mur.

ALSO: Coenzyme Q10, Bee pollen granules or tablets. Pollen-rich unprocessed raw honey.

REFERENCES:
Vitamin Bible - E. Mindell
References listed for "Allergies".

HEADACHE.....
HOMEOPATHIC COMBINATION (Tension Headache Formula)

SINGLE HERBS: Chamomile and Feverfew.

VITAMINS: A, B1, B2, B3, B6, B12, B complex, C, D, E, and F.
MINERALS: Calcium, Magnesium, Potassium, and Zinc.
ESSENTIAL OILS: Lavender and Peppermint.
FLOWER REMEDIES: Take Bachs Rescue Remedy.
TISSUE SALTS: Ferr phos, Kali phos, and Mag Phos.
ALSO: Acidophilus, and Q10.
REFERENCES:
The Complete Natural Health Encyclopedia - David Nyholt
Natural Treatments and Remedies - Global Health

HEEL SPUR . . . . .
SINGLE HERBS: ..
VITAMINS: B complex, B6, and C.
MINERALS: Calcium and Magnesium.
TISSUE SALTS: Mag phos.
ALSO: Bioflavonoids and Proteolytic enzymes.
REFERENCES:
The Complete Natural Health Encyclopedia - David Nyholt

HEART BURN . . . . .
HERBAL COMBINATION:
(Motion Mate)
SINGLE HERBS: Chamomile, Chewable Papaya, Meadowsweet, and Marshmallow Root.
ESSENTIAL OILS: Bergamot, Dill Lavender, and Ylang-Ylang.
FLOWER REMEDIES: Combine Holly, Hornbeam, and Impatiens.
ALSO: Digestive enzymes (especially Pancreatic enzymes), bone meal, and primadophilus

HEART DISEASE . . . . .
HERBAL COMBINATIONS: (H)
(Garlicin HC)
PHYSIOLOGIC ACTION: Promotes elasticity of arteries. Helps eliminate cholesterol, also aids in rebuilding the heart, strengthening and regulating the beat of the heart, and improving circulation in general.
SINGLE HERBS: Barberry, Cayenne, Garlic, Hawthorn Berries, Lobelia, and Shepherds Purse.
VITAMINS: A, B1, B5, B15, C, D, E, Lecithin, Biotin, Inositol, Choline, and Folic Acid.
MINERALS: Calcium, Copper, Iodine, Iron, Magnesium, and Potassium.
ESSENTIAL OILS: Basil, Lavender, Pine, and Thyme.
FLOWER REMEDIES: Combine Beech, Holly, Impatiens, Mustard, and Willow.
TISSUE SALTS: Calc phos, Ferr phos, Kali phos, and Nat sulph.
REFERENCES:
Heart and Vitamin E - Shute
How to Get Well - P. Airola

HEMORRHOIDS . . . . .
HERBAL COMBINATION:
(Yellow Dock Formula)
PHYSIOLOGIC ACTION:
Effective formula for hemorrhoids, colitis and blood purifier. Also revitalizes prolapsed uterus, kidneys and bowl.
SINGLE HERBS: Butchers Broom, Collinsonia Root, Horsechestnut, Lobelia, Stone Root, and Yellow Dock.
VITAMINS: A, B6, B Complex, C, E, P, and Vit E oil.
MINERALS: Multi-mineral plus Calcium.
ESSENTIAL OILS: Cypress, Garlic, Juniper, and Tea Tree Oil.
FLOWER REMEDIES: Beech, Cherry Plum, and Crabapple.
TISSUE SALTS: Calc fluor, Ferr phos, and Mag phos.

ALSO: Bulk forming laxatives such as Laxacil, or Psyllium seed husks are recommended to take pressure from the colon. Combination "Hem Relief" ointment, Pile ointment and suppositories or Circu Caps Witch Hazel Compresses.
REFERENCES:
How to Get Well - P. Airola
Vitamin Bible - E. Mindell

HERPES SIMPLEX (1&2)

SINGLE HERBS: Echinacea, Goldenseal. Myrrh, Red Clover, and Turkish Rhubarb.
VITAMINS: B complex, C, and E.
MINERALS: Zinc chelate.
ESSENTIAL OILS: Basil, Bergamot, Camphor, Melissa, and Tea Tree Oil.
FLOWER REMEDIES: Combine Holly, Hornbeam, Impatiens, and Mimulus.
TISSUE SALTS: Calc sulph, Ferr phos, and Kali phos.
ALSO: Canaid herbal drink.
REFERENCES:
The Complete Natural Health Encyclopedia - David Nyholt
Drugs and Beyond - David Nyholt

HIATAL HERNIA .....

SINGLE HERBS: Aloe Vera Juice, Comfrey, Goldenseal, and Red Clover.
VITAMINS: A, B12, B Complex, and C.
MINERALS: Multi-Mineral plus Zinc
ESSENTIAL OILS: Bergamot, Lavender, Neroli, and Peppermint.
FLOWER REMEDIES: Aspen, Gorse, and Holly.
TISSUE SALTS: Calc phos, Ferr phos, Mag phos, and Nat phos..
ALSO: Pancreatin, Papaya, and Proteolytic Enzymes.

REFERENCES:
The Complete Natural Health Encyclopedia - David Nyholt
Natural Treatments and Remedies -Global Health

HIV DISEASE .....
Refer to *Aids* **Page 11**

HIVES .....
Refer to *Allergies* **Page 11**

HORMONE REGULATION .....

FEMALE HERB COMBINATION: (MP) or (Change-O-Life)
PHYSIOLOGIC ACTION: This herbal formula is effective in regulating hormonal imbalance. Its greatest benefit is for the relief of the symptoms of menopause. Also good for youth during puberty.
SINGLE HERBS: Blessed Thistle, Damiana, Dong Quai, Mistletoe, and Vitex Agnus Castus
MALE HERB COMBINATION: (APH)
PHYSIOLOGIC ACTION: Stimulates sexual impulses, strengthens and increases sexual power. Help eliminate fatigue and increases longevity.
SINGLE HERBS: Damiana, Fo-Ti, Gota Kola, Sarsaparilla Root, Saw Palmetto, and Siberian Ginseng.
MINERALS: Potassium.
ESSENTIAL OILS: Clary Sage, Fennel, Geranium, and Sage.
REFERENCES:
Herbally Yours - P. Royal
Every Woman's Book - P. Airola
Health Through God's Pharmacy

HORMONE IMBALANCE .....
Refer to *Menopause* **Page 35**

HOUSEMAID'S KNEE ...

HERBAL COMBINATIONS:
(Rheum- Aid) (Cal-Silica) (Kalmin)
PHYSIOLOGIC ACTION: These herbal combinations contain herbs which exhibit anti-inflammatory and relaxing effects. Help to build nerve tissue and relieve stiffness and pain.
SINGLE HERBS: Alfalfa, Chaparral, and Comfrey.
VITAMINS: A, B12, B complex, C, E, and P.
MINERALS: Calcium, Magnesium.
ALSO: Alkaline diet, Coenzyme Q10, Germanium, and Protein supplements.
REFERENCES:
The Complete Natural Health Encyclopedia - David Nyholt
Natural Treatments and Remedies

HYPERACTIVITY .....

HERBAL COMBINATION: (Wild Lettuce and Valerian Extract)
PHYSIOLOGIC ACTION: This excellent formula is a natural sedative. Promotes overall calming of the nerves and restores a sense of control and balance without causing drowsiness.
ALSO: Ginkgo or Ginkgold. Although this herb is often used to promote circulation, it also has a positive effect on the nervous system, Used in conjunction with the following single herbs, and with a balanced, chemical free diet, good results can be expected.
SINGLE HERBS: Evening Primrose Oil Lobelia, Oat Extract, Skullcap, St. Johns Wort, Valerian, and Wild Lettuce.
VITAMINS: High potency B vitamins, B3, B5, B6, and C.

NOTE: Yeast free B vitamins may be required if yeast intolerance is present.
MINERALS: High doses of all minerals.
ESSENTIAL OILS: Lavender, Neroli, Chamomile, and Rose.
FLOWER REMEDIES: Combine Cherry Plum, Impatiens, and Vervain.
TISSUE SALTS: Ferr phos and Kali phos.
Note: avoid all foods with artificial flavoring and coloring. Processed foods should be eliminated from the diet. Foods which contain natural salicylates such as apples, and oranges need to be avoided.
REFERENCES:
The Hyperactive Child - Barnes and Colquhoun.

HYPERTHYROIDISM ...

HERBAL COMBINATIONS: (GL) (IF)
PHYSIOLOGIC ACTIONS:
Effective for swollen lymph nodes and in helping the body fight glandular weakness and infections.
SINGLE HERBS: Alfalfa, Calendula, Echinacea, Golden Seal, Lobelia, Mullein, Saw Palmetto, and Skullcap.
VITAMINS: A, B5, B Complex (stress), C, and E.
MINERALS: Calcium, Magnesium, and Potassium.
ESSENTIAL OILS: Lavender and Rosemary.
FLOWER REMEDIES: Combine Holly, Impatiens, and White Chestnut.
ALSO: Multi Glandulars and Primrose Oil.
REFERENCES:
Herbally Yours - P. Royal
Natural Treatments and Remedies - Global Health

HYPOGLYCEMIA.....

HERBAL COMBINATIONS:
(HIGL) (AdrenAid)

PHYSIOLOGIC ACTION: Stimulates the adrenals and the pancreas to help restore sugar levels, helps correct glandular imbalances, eliminates toxins, assists the body in handling stress conditions and promotes a feeling of well being.
Note: Some people who have hypoglycemia cannot handle Golden Seal, as it tends to lower the blood sugar. Safflower is good to take before exercise.

VITAMINS: A, B3, B complex, C, E, and Folic Acid.

MINERALS: Magnesium, and Potassium.

ESSENTIAL OILS: Eucalyptus and Fennel.

FLOWER REMEDIES: Holly and Impatiens.

ALSO: Bee Pollen, Juniper, Glycolite, Acidophilus. Low animal protein, small meals high in natural complex carbohydrates.

REFERENCES:
Hypoglycemia - P. Airola
How to Get Well - P Airola
Vitamin Bible - E. Mindell

HYPOTENSION.....

Refer to *Blood Pressure Low* Page 16

HYPOTHYROIDISM....

HERBAL COMBINATION: (T)

PHYSIOLOGIC ACTION: An excellent formula to help revitalize and promote healing of the thyroid glands, thus restoring metabolism balance.

SINGLE HERBS: Black Walnut, Irish Moss, Kelp, and Mullein.

VITAMINS: A, B1, B5, C, D, E, and F.

MINERALS: Calcium, Magnesium, and Potassium.

ESSENTIAL OILS: Lemon and Palmarosa.

FLOWER REMEDIES: Combine Larch, Olive, and Scleranthus.

ALSO: Brewers Yeast, Essential Fatty Acids, Protein, and Thyroid Glandular.

REFERENCES:
Glandular Extracts - Donsbach
Herbally Yours - P. Royal
Natural Treatments and Remedies - Global Health
The Complete Natural Health Encyclopedia - David Nyholt

IMPETIGO.....

HERBAL COMBINATIONS: (Red Clover Combination) (Yellow Dock Formula) (AKN)

PHYSIOLOGIC ACTION: These herbal formulas effectively aid the body's cleansing systems thus helps eliminate ulcers of the skin, impetigo etc.

SINGLE HERBS: Echinacea, Licorice Root and Red Clover.

VITAMINS: A, C, D, E. Vitamin A and E applied topically. Vitamin A is necessary for the health of the skin tissue, and vitamins C, D, and E, may be helpful in aiding the skin in its recovery from impetigo.

ESSENTIAL OILS: Tea Tree Oil.

REFERENCES:
Back to Eden - J. Kloss
Nutrition Almanac

IMMUNE DEFICIENCY

HERBAL COMBINATION:
(Echina Guard)

PHYSIOLOGIC ACTION: Stimulates the immune response systems. Especially helpful in rebuilding the body during convalescence and as a preventative.

SINGLE HERBS: Echinacea Root, Chaparral, Korean White Ginseng, Pau d' Arco, Rosemary, and Golden Seal Root.
VITAMINS: A Multi-vitamin plus B6, B12, C, and E.
MINERALS: A strong complete multi - time release
ESSENTIAL OILS: Cajeput, Garlic, Lavender, and Niaouli.
FLOWER REMEDIES: Aspen, Mustard, Mimulus, and Rock Rose.
TISSUE SALTS: Calc phos, Kali phos, and Silicea.
ALSO: Canaid herbal Drink, L-Cysteine, L-Methionine, L-Lysine, L-Ornithine, Propolis and Primadophilus.

IMPOTENCE . . . . .

HERBAL COMBINATION: (APH)
PHYSIOLOGIC ACTION: Stimulates male and female sexual impulses as well as strengthens and increases sexual power and helps fight fatigue.
SINGLE HERBS: Damiana, Gotu Kola, Ginkgo, Ginseng, Potency Wood, and Puncture Vine.
VITAMINS: E, Paba, Folic Acid, and Lecithin.
MINERALS: Zinc, Iodine, and Calcium.
ESSENTIAL OILS: Anise, Jasmine Juniper, Rose, and Ylang-Ylang.
FLOWER REMEDIES: Take Bachs Rescue Remedy.
ALSO: Melbrosia (for men), Tropical Impulse tea, and Loving Mood.
ALSO: Sesame Seeds, Ginseng, Damiana, high quality vegetable oil, fertile eggs, and raw milk.
REFERENCES:
Herbally Yours - P. Royal
Drugs and Beyond - David Nyholt
The Complete Natural Health Encyclopedia - David Nyholt.
How to Get Well - P. Airola

INCONTINENCE . . . . .

HERBAL COMBINATION: (KB).
PHYSIOLOGIC ACTION:
Extremely valuable in healing and strengthening the kidneys, bladder, and genito-urinary area.
SINGLE HERBS: Alfalfa, Barberry root, Catnip, Horsetail, Ginger Root, Goldenrod, and Uva Ursi.
VITAMINS: A, B complex, C, D, and E.
MINERALS: Calcium, Magnesium, and Potassium.
ESSENTIAL OILS: Bergamot, Tea Tree, and Thyme.
FLOWER REMEDIES: Mimulus and Wild Oat.
TISSUE SALTS: Calc phos, Ferr phos, Kali phos, and Nat mur.
ALSO: Digestive enzymes, Diuretic tablets, Lecithin, L-Arginine, L-Methionine, Propolis, and Uratonic.

INDIGESTION . . . . .

Refer to *Digestive Disorders* Page 29

INFERTILITY . . . . .

SINGLE HERBS: Dong Qui and Gotu Kola.
VITAMINS: A, B6, B Complex, and E.
MINERALS: A Complete Mineral Complex.
ESSENTIAL OILS: Jasmine, Lavender, and Rose.
FLOWER REMEDIES:
(For-Women) Beech, Elm, Holly, Impatiens, Mustard, and White Chestnut.
(For-Men) Oak and White Chestnut
ALSO: Astrelin, Gerovital H3, L-Tyrosine, Proteolytic Enzymes, and Raw Ovarian Concentrate.
REFERENCES:
Natural Treatments and Remedies

The Complete Natural Health Encyclopedia - David Nyholt

INFLUENZA .....
Refer to *Colds and Flu* **Page 24**

INSOMNIA .....
HERBAL COMBINATIONS: (E-Z Sleep) (Silent Night)
PHYSIOLOGIC ACTION: Soothing mild relaxant. Promotes natural restful and refreshing sleep.
SINGLE HERBS: Catnip, Hops, Skullcap, Pau d'Arco, and Valerian Root.
VITAMINS: B1, B3, B, B6, D, and E.
MINERALS: Calcium, Iron, Magnesium, and Potassium
ESSENTIAL OILS: Lavender, Neroli, and Ylang-Ylang.
FLOWER REMEDIES: Combine Cherry Plum, Gorse, and Mustard.
TISSUE SALTS: Kali phos, Mag phos, and Nat mur.
ALSO: Taheebo, Protein, and Tryptophan.
REFERENCES:
Amino Acids Book - C. Wade

INTESTINAL PARASITES .....
Refer to *Parasites* **Page 53**

IRRITABLE BLADDER .
Refer to *Kidney and Bladder* **Page 43**

JAUNDICE (NON INFECTIOUS) ....
HERBAL COMBINATION: (LG)
PHYSIOLOGIC ACTION: This herbal combination helps to correct malfunctioning of the liver and gall bladder. It is a liver detoxifier, and a bile stimulant.

SINGLE HERBS: Birch Leaves, Dandelion, Fennel, Horse Tail, Irish Moss, and Rose Hips.
VITAMINS: A, B6, C, D, and E.
MINERALS: Calcium, Magnesium and Phosphorus.
ESSENTIAL OILS: Orange and Rosemary.
FLOWER REMEDIES: Combine Holly, Impatiens, Wild Oat, and Willow.
TISSUE SALTS: Ferr phos, Kali mur, Kali sulph, and Nat sulph.
ALSO: Lecithin, Protein, and Unsaturated fatty acids.
REFERENCES:
How to Get Well - P. Airola
The Nature Doctor - A. Vogel

JET LAG .....
SPECIFIC: Siberian ginseng, taken on a regular bases for about a week before the trip, seems to have a balancing effect on the system, lessening the effects of Jet Lag. A good vitamin supplement is also helpful.
SINGLE HERBS: Gota kola, Korean Ginseng.
VITAMINS: Stress B Complex, Multi-Vitamin, C, and E.
MINERALS: A Multi-mineral complex.
REFERENCES:
Vitamin Bible - E. Mindell

KIDNEY - BLADDER DISORDERS .....
HERBAL COMBINATION: (KB)
PHYSIOLOGIC ACTION: Extremely valuable in healing and strengthening the kidneys, bladder and genito-urinary area. Useful to stop bed wetting, but is a diuretic when congestion of the kidneys is indicated. Helps remove bladder, uterine and urethral toxins.

Warning: Intended for occasional use only. May cause green-yellow discoloration of urine.

SINGLE HERBS: Alfalfa, Catnip, Dandelion, Fennel, Goldenrod, Horsetail, Uva Ursi, and Wild Yam.

VITAMINS: A, B complex, C, D, E, and Choline.

MINERALS: Calcium, Magnesium, and Potassium.

ESSENTIAL OILS: Tea Tree Oil.

FLOWER REMEDIES: Hornbean, Impatiens, Mimulus, and Mustard.

TISSUE SALTS: Ferr phos, Kali phos, and Kali Mur.

ALSO: Cranberry juice, Propolis, Uratonic, Watermelon, 3-way herb teas, and other Diuretic tablets

REFERENCES:
Own Your Own Body - S. Malstom
Lets Get Well - A. Davis
How to Get Well - P. Airola

KIDNEY FAILURE .....

SINGLE HERBS: Garlic and Parsley.

PHYSIOLOGIC ACTION: Promotes urine flow and strengthens kidneys. Also revitalizes and strengthens liver and spleen.

ALSO: Propolis, Cranberry juice, 3-way herb teas, and Uratonic.
Refer to Kidney and Bladder in this manual.

REFERENCES:
"Diets to Help Cystitis"—McCutcheon
Back to Eden - J. Kloss

KIDNEY - BLADDER STONES .....

HERBAL COMBINATION: (PR)

PHYSIOLOGIC ACTION: PR comb helps dissolve kidney stones. PR helps keep kidneys flushed out (toxins and buildup of waste and sediments). Juniper keeps kidneys flushed out. Parsley acts as a diuretic. Magnesium helps prevent stones from forming. Thyme helps prevent buildup and dissolves stones if already present.

SINGLE HERBS: Corn silk, Dandelion, Juniper, Parsley, Thyme, and Uva Ursi.

VITAMINS: A, B2, B5, B6, C, E, F, and Choline.

MINERALS: Magnesium, and Potassium.

ESSENTIAL OILS: Fennel, Geranium, and Roman Chamomile.

FLOWER REMEDIES: Hornbean, Impatiens, Mimulus and Mustard.

TISSUE SALTS: Ferr phos.

ALSO: Apple Juice, Lemon Juice, and Marshmallow.

REFERENCES:
How to Get Well - P. Airola
Health Through God's Pharmacy - M. Treben

LABOR AND DELIVERY .....

SINGLE HERB: Red Raspberry.

PHYSIOLOGIC ACTION: Red Raspberry is essential during labor. It coordinates the uterine contractions often making labor shorter.

REFERENCES:
Herbally Yours - P. Royal

LARYNGITIS .....
Refer to *Sore Throat* Page 44

LEG CRAMPS .....
(Charley Horse)

HERBAL COMBINATION: (Ca-T)

PHYSIOLOGIC ACTION: Effectively clams nerves and aids sleep in addition to rebuilding the nerve sheath, vein and artery walls.

SINGLE HERBS: Comfrey Herb, Horsetail Grass, Oat Straw, and Skullcap.
VITAMINS: B complex, B5, C, D, and E.
MINERALS: Calcium, Magnesium and Phosphorus.
ESSENTIAL OILS: Chamomile, Geranium, and Lavender.
FLOWER REMEDIES: Take Bachs Rescue Remedy.
TISSUE SALTS: Calc phos, Kali phos, and Mag phos.
ALSO: #12 tissue salts
REFERENCES:
Calcium Bible - P. Hausman
Vitamin Bible - E. Mindell

LEG ULCERS .....

HERBAL COMBINATION: (H Formula) or (Ginkgold)
PHYSIOLOGIC ACTION: Strengthens the heart and builds the vascular system.
SINGLE HERBS: Cayenne, Bayberry, Butchers Broom, Ginkgo, and Yarrow.
VITAMINS: A, B3, B12, C, and E.
MINERALS: Calcium, Iron, Magnesium, and Potassium.
ESSENTIAL OILS: Geranium, Lavender, and Myrrh.
FLOWER REMEDIES: Chicory, Crabapple, and Impatiens.
TISSUE SALTS: Calc Fluor, Ferr phos, and Silicea.
ALSO: Coenzyme Q10, Germanium
REFERENCES:
Herbally Yours - P. Royal

LEUKEMIA .....

SINGLE HERBS: Pau d'Arco, Swedish Bitters, and Nettle.
VITAMINS: B complex, B12, C, and E.
MINERALS: Copper, Iron, and Zinc.
Refer to "Cancer" in the manual

ESSENTIAL OILS: Basil, Carrot Seed, Elemi, Geranium, Hyssop, Tarragon, Tea Tree, and Violet.
FLOWER REMEDIES: Take Bachs Rescue Remedy.
TISSUE SALTS: Calc phos and Kali phos.
REFERENCES:
Nutrition Almanac - J. Kirschmann

LEUKORRHEA .....

HERBAL COMBINATION: (Cantrol)
PHYSIOLOGIC ACTION: An excellent well-balanced formula of herbs and supplements which balance the system while killing yeast.
SINGLE HERBS: Black Walnut, Caprinex, Garlic, Pau d' Arco, and Yucca.
VITAMINS: A, B Complex, Biotin, D, and E.
MINERALS: Calcium and Magnesium.
ESSENTIAL OILS: Tea Tree Oil.
FLOWER REMEDIES: Combine Holly, Impatiens, and White Chestnut.
ALSO: Yu-ccan Herbal Drink, Linseed Oil, Candida Cleanse, Caprilic Acid, and Primadophilus.
REFERENCES:
Herbally Yours - P. Royal
Natural Treatments and Remedies
The Complete Natural Health Encyclopedia - David Nyholt

LIBITO PROBLEMS ....

Refer to *Impotence* Page 42

LIVER AND GALLBLADDER .....

HERBAL COMBINATION: (LG)
PHYSIOLOGIC ACTION: Helps the cleansing of the liver and gall bladder, restores new energy to

these organs. Also can be taken to relieve intestinal gas.

SINGLE HERBS: Bayberry Root, Catnip, Fennel Seed, Ginger Root, and Peppermint.

VITAMINS: A, B1, B2, B6, Choline, Niacin, Pantothenic Acid, C, and E.

MINERALS: Copper and Sulfur for the Liver. Magnesium and Sulfur for the Gallbladder.

ESSENTIAL OILS: Juniper, Lemon, Lime, Tangerine, and Roman Chamomile.

FLOWER REMEDIES: Combine Gorse, Holly, and Impatiens.

TISSUE SALTS: Nat sulph.

ALSO: Acidophlis, Carrot juice, Calamus Root tea, Chlorophyll, and all green drinks.

REFERENCES:
The Master Cleanser- S. Burroughs
Health Through God's Pharmacy - M. Treben

LIVER DISEASES . . . . .

HERBAL COMBINATIONS:
(Thisilyn) — (Milk Thistle Extract)

PHYSIOLOGIC ACTION: Protects liver. Anti-oxidant quality prevents free radical damage in the liver.

SINGLE HERBS: Dandelion and Horsetail.

VITAMINS: A, B Complex, B1, B2, B3, B6, C, E, Choline, and Lecithin.

FLOWER REMEDIES: Impatiens.

TISSUE SALTS: Kali mur, and Nat phos.

ALSO: Digestive Enzymes, and Primadophilus.

REFERENCES:
How to Get Well - P. Airola
Drugs and Beyond - David Nyholt
The Complete Natural Health Encyclopedia - David Nyholt.
Nutrition Almanac - J. Kirschmann

LOWER BOWEL PROBLEMS . . . . .

HERBAL COMBINATIONS:
(Multilax #2) or (Naturalax #2)

PHYSIOLOGIC ACTION: Accelerates natural cleansing of the body and improves intestinal absorption by gentle evacuation of bowls. Cleans out old toxic fecal matter, mucus and encrustation's from the colon wall and helps normalize the peristaltic action and rebuild the bowel structure. Use until the bowel is cleansed, healed and functioning normally.

SINGLE HERBS: Calamus Root, Golden Seal Root, Lobelia, Red Raspberry, Eucarbon, and Yucca..

VITAMINS: A Muiti-vitamin plus a B Complex.

MINERALS: A strong Multi-mineral Complex.

ESSENTIAL OILS: Cumin, Fennel, Marjoram, and Pepper.

ALSO: Yu-ccan herbal drink, Flax Seeds, Psyllium Seeds, and Figs.

REFERENCES:
Colon Health - Dr. N. Walker
Health Through God's Pharmacy - M. Treben

LUMBAGO . . . . .
Refer to *Back Pain* Page 14

LUNG CANCER . . . . .
Refer to *Cancer* Page 21

MASTITIS . . . . .

VITAMINS: A good multi-vitamin, plus B complex, C, and D.

MINERALS: Calcium, Manganese, and Iron.

FLOWER REMEDIES: Take Bachs Rescue Remedy.

TISSUE SALTS: Ferr phos, Kali mur, and Silicea.

ALSO: Acidophlus and protein.
REFERENCES:
The Complete Natural Health Encyclopedia - David Nyholt

MEASLES . . . . .

HERBAL COMBINATION: (Fenu-Thyme) or (ANT-PLG Syrup).
PHYSIOLOGIC ACTION: Acts as a support to the immune system.
SINGLE HERBS: Garlic, Catnip tea, Turkey Rhubarb, and Pau d Arco.
VITAMINS: A, C, and E.
MINERALS: Calcium, Magnesium, and Zinc.
ESSENTIAL OILS: Benzoin, Lavender, Rose, and Ylang-Ylang.
FLOWER REMEDIES: Take Bachs Rescue Remedy.
TISSUE SALTS: Calc phos, Ferr phos, Kali Mur, and Silicea.
ALSO: Raw thymus and Proteolytic enzymes.
REFERENCES:
"The Complete Natural Health Encyclopedia"—David Nyholt

MELANOMA . . . . .

SINGLE HERBS: Kelp and Pau d' Arco.
VITAMINS: A, B Complex, B12, Niacin, Folic Acid, C, and E.
MINERALS: A strong Multi-mineral plus Calcium, Magnesium, and Potassium.
ESSENTIAL OILS: Borneol, Cypress, Hyssop, Tarragon, Tea Tree, and Violet.
FLOWER REMEDIES: Take Bachs Rescue Remedy.
ALSO: Coenzyme Q10, Germanium, L-Cysteine, L-Methionine, L-Taurine, Essential Fatty Acids, Primadophilus, Proteolytic Enzymes and Raw Glandular Complex with extra Raw Thymus

REFERENCES:
Glandular Extracts - Donsbach
The Complete Natural Health Encyclopedia - David Nyholt

MEMORY LOSS . . . . .

HERBAL COMBINATIONS: (SEN) or (Remem)
PHYSIOLOGIC ACTION: This formula contains remarkable rejuvenating properties that nourish the brain cells and tissues and improves their ability to perform mental functions.
SINGLE HERBS: Cayenne, Ginkgo, Gotu Kola, Korean Ginseng, and Lobelia.
VITAMINS: Choline, and Lecithin.
MINERALS: Multi-mineral complex.
ESSENTIAL OILS: Basil, Peppermint, and Rosemary.
FLOWER REMEDIES: Impatiens.
TISSUE SALTS: Calc phos and Nat mur.
REFERENCES:
Mental Alertness - Donsbach
Drugs and Beyond - David Nyholt
Vitamin Bible - E. Mindell

MENINGITIS . . . . .

SINGLE HERBS: Catnip and Garlic.
VITAMINS: Multi-vitamin plus A, C, and D.
MINERALS: A high potency mineral complex, plus Calcium, and Zinc.
FLOWER REMEDIES: Take Bachs Rescue Remedy.
ALSO: Germanium, Protein, and Raw Thymus.
REFERENCES:
Natural Treatments and Remedies
The Complete Natural Health Encyclopedia - David Nyholt

MENOPAUSE .....

HERBAL COMBINATIONS:
(Change-O-Life) or (MP)
PHYSIOLOGIC ACTION: For both male and female health to the pancreas, pituitary and other glandular areas and maintains a healthy hormone balance in the body, especially during puberty and menopause.
Warning: not intended for use during pregnancy
SINGLE HERBS: Black Cohosh, Blessed Thistle, Licorice Root, Sarsaparilla, and Siberian Ginseng,
VITAMINS: A, B complex, B3, C, D, and E.
MINERALS: Calcium, magnesium, Potassium, and Selenium.
ESSENTIAL OILS: Geranium, Lavender, and Peppermint.
FLOWER REMEDIES: Combine Aspen, Centaury, Cerato, Mimulus, Sweet Chestnut, and White Chestnut.
TISSUE SALTS: Calc phos and Kali phos.
ALSO: Melbrosia, Damiana, Germanium, Quan Yin, and Ginseng.
REFERENCES:
Every Woman's Book - P. Airola
Vitamin Bible - E. Mindell

MENSTRUATION .....

HERBAL COMBINATIONS: (FC) or (FEM-MEND)
PHYSIOLOGIC ACTION: Helps regulate the menstrual cycle, relieve cramps, bloating and vaginitis, ease inflammation of the vagina and uterus, and strengthen and regulate the kidneys, bladder and uterus areas. Beneficial for all female and uterine complaints.
Warning: Do not use this combination while taking estrogen or oral contraceptives.
SINGLE HERBS: Red Raspberry, and Uva Ursi.
VITAMINS: B complex, B6, C, E, and Iodine.
ESSENTIAL OILS: Clary Sage, Cypress, and Lavender.
TISSUE SALTS: Ferr phos and Kali phos.
REFERENCES:
Every Woman's Book - P. Airola
The Complete Natural Health Encyclopedia - David Nyholt.
PMS Book - Wade

MIGRAINE HEADACHES .....

PHYSIOLOGIC ACTION: Camomile will prevent migraine headaches. Feverfew reduces fever. Feverfew has been historically used for chills and pain that accompany fever. Because of its anecdotal claims for cluster or migraine suffers, it is presently being researched at the London Migraine Clinic.
SINGLE HERBS: Camomile, Feverfew, Ginkgo, and Yucca.
VITAMINS: B3, B5, B12, B Complex, C, F, Paba, and Niacin.
MINERALS: Calcium, Magnesium, and Potassium.
ESSENTIAL OILS: Peppermint.
FLOWER REMEDIES: Take Bachs Rescue Remedy.
TISSUE SALTS: Calc phos, Kali phos, and Nat mur.
ALSO: Unsaturated fatty acids.
REFERENCES:
Feverfew Your Headache may be Over - Hancock
Herbally Yours - P. Royal
How to Get Well - P. Airola

MONONUCLEOSIS . . . . .

VITAMINS: A, B complex, B1, B2, B5, B6, C, Biotin, and Choline.
MINERALS: Potassium.
ESSENTIAL OILS: Elemi, Myrrh, Pine, and Wild Oat.
FLOWER REMEDIES: Combine Holly, Impatiens, and Wild Oat.
TISSUE SALTS: Nat mur.
ALSO: Canaid herbal drink, Germanium, Raw thymus, Raw Glandular Complex, and Protein.
REFERENCES:
Natural Treatments and Remedies
Vitamin Bible - E. Mindell

MORNING SICKNESS . .

SINGLE HERBS: Red Raspberry or Peppermint Tea often overcomes nausea. Alfalfa, Catnip, & Ginger tea may also be helpful. Sometimes small frequent meals instead of a larger one is beneficial.
VITAMINS: A Multi-vitamin plus B6, C, and K.
MINERALS: Multi-mineral.
TISSUE SALTS: Nat mur and Nat phos.
ALSO: Avoid cigarette smoke, alcohol, white sugar, refined carbohydrates, coffee, and other stimulants.
Note: Morning sickness may be due to either an intolerance or a deficiency.

MOTION SICKNESS . . . .

HERBAL COMBINATION:
(Motion Mate)
PHYSIOLOGIC ACTION: In a recent university study ginger root caps proved more effective than either a drug or placebo at controlling motion induced nausea, also queasy travelers have found taking B complex at night and just before the trip is most effective.
SINGLE HERBS: Ginger Root Caps.
VITAMINS: B complex plus B6.
MINERALS: Magnesium.
ESSENTIAL OILS: Ginger and Peppermint.
TISSUE SALTS: Kali phos and Nat phos.
ALSO: Charcoal tablets.
REFERENCES:
Vitamin Bible - E. Mindell
Drugs and Beyond - David Nyholt.
Original Herb Formulas - L. Griffin

MOUTH SORES . . . . .
(Canker, Thrush, and Pyorrhea)
SINGLE HERBS: Aloe Vera, Golden Seal, Myrrh, Red Raspberry, and White Oak Bark.
VITAMINS: A, B2, B3, B12, B Complex, C, and E..
MINERALS: Iron, Magnesium, Phosphorus, and Zinc.
ESSENTIAL OILS: Geranium and Lavender.
FLOWER REMEDIES: Impatiens.
TISSUE SALTS: Silicea.
ALSO: Chlorophyll, Lysine, and Primadophilus.
REFERENCES:
Bee Medicine - Uccusic
Healing Power of Chlorophyll - Jensen

MULTIPLE SCLEROSIS . . . . .

SINGLE HERBS: Evening Primrose Oil, Kelp, Oat Extract, Skullcap, and St.John's Wort.
VITAMINS: B complex, B1, B2, B3, B5, B6, B12, C, E, F, Inositol, and Lecithin.
MINERALS: Calcium, Copper, Iron, Magnesium, Manganese, Selenium, and Zinc.

ESSENTIAL OILS: Carrot Seed, Clove, Tarragon, and Tea Tree Oil.
FLOWER REMEDIES: Combine Beech, Chicory, Gorse, Holly, and Hornbean.
ALSO: Bonemeal, Coenzyme Q10, Germanium, L-Leucine, L-Isoleucine, L-Valine, Protein, and Digestive Enzymes.
REFERENCES:
How to Get Well - P. Airola
Nutrition Almanac - J. Kirschmann

MUMPS .....

HERBAL COMBINATION: (ANT-PLG)
PHYSIOLOGIC ACTION: An effective formula that helps cleanse toxins and reduce infection. This combination is a natural aid in fighting contagious diseases.
SINGLE HERBS: Bayberry Root Bark, Echinacea, Ginger Root, Lobelia, and Mullein.
VITAMINS: A, B Complex, C, E.
MINERALS: A complete multi complex.
ESSENTIAL OILS: Peppermint.
FLOWER REMEDIES: Take Bachs Rescue Remedy.
TISSUE SALTS: Kali mur.
ALSO: Germanium and Acidophilus.

MUSCLE INJURIES ....
Refer to *Athletic Injuries* P 14

MUSCULAR DYSTROPHY .....

SINGLE HERBS: Saw Palmetto.
VITAMINS: A, B complex, B3, B5, B6, B12, C, E, and Choline.
MINERALS: Potassium.
ALSO: Protein and Unsaturated fatty acids.
REFERENCES:
How to Get Well - P. Airola

Nutrition Almanac - J. Kirschmann

MYOCARDIAL INFARCTION .....

HERBAL COMBINATION: (Garlicin HC)
PHYSIOLOGIC ACTION: Strengthens the heart, cleanses arteries and veins, and builds the vascular system.
SINGLE HERBS: Cayenne, Comfrey, Evening Primrose Oil, Fish Oil, Garlic, Golden Seal, and Rose Hips.
VITAMINS: B Complex, C, E, Niacin, Inositol, and Choline.
MINERALS: Calcium and Magnesium.
ESSENTIAL OILS: Elemi for stress and Basil for circulation.
FLOWER REMEDIES: Take Bachs Rescue Remedy and Willow.
ALSO: Coenzyme Q10, L-Carnitine, L-Cysteine, L-Methionine, Multidigestive Enzymes, DMG, Fish Oils, and Vegetable Oils.
REFERENCES:
Natural Treatments & Remedies
The Complete Natural Health Encyclopedia - David Nyholt

MYXEDEMA .....
Refer to *Hypothyroidism* P 50

NAUSEA – VOMITING ..

HERBAL COMBINATION: (Herbal Influence)
PHYSIOLOGIC ACTION: Contains herbs which help with fever and nausea.
SINGLE HERBS: Cayenne, Chaparral, Garlic, Raspberry, Red Clover, Rose Hips, Golden Seal.
VITAMINS: A, B6, C, and P.
MINERALS: Magnesium.
ESSENTIAL OILS: Peppermint and Lavender.

FLOWER REMEDIES: Take Bachs Rescue Remedy.
TISSUE SALTS: Kali phos, Nat mur, and Nat phos.
REFERENCES:
Global Herb Manual - Z Fortisevn
The Complete Natural Health Encyclopedia - David Nyholt

NERVOUSNESS .....
(Tension - Anxiety)
HERBAL COMBINATIONS:
(Calm-aid) or (Ex stress comb)
PHYSIOLOGIC ACTION: A proven formula that is soothing, strengthening and healing to the whole nervous system to relieve nervous tension and rebuild the nerve sheaths. Excellent aid for insomnia, chronic nervousness and stress-related conditions.
SINGLE HERBS: Evening Primrose Oil, Hops, Mistletoe, Skullcap, and Valerian.
VITAMINS: B complex, B1, B2, B3, B5, B6, and C.
MINERALS: Calcium, Iodine, Iron, Magnesium, Phosphorus, Potassium, Silicon, and Sodium.
ESSENTIAL OILS: .Chamomile, Eucalyptus, Geranium, and Pine.
FLOWER REMEDIES: Take Bachs Rescue Remedy.
TISSUE SALTS: Kali phos and Nat mur.
REFERENCES:
Stress Without Distress - Selye
Drugs and Beyond - David Nyholt.
Stress - Donsbach

NETTLE RASH .....
SINGLE HERBS: Evening Primrose and Tea Tree Oil..
VITAMINS: C and E.
MINERALS: A multi-mineral.
ESSENTIAL OILS: Chamomile, Lavender, and Rosemary.

FLOWER REMEDIES: Impatiens.
TISSUE SALTS: Ferr phos and Nat mur.
ALSO: Pantothenic acid.
REFERENCES:
The Complete Natural Health Encyclopedia - David Nyholt

NEURITIS .....
SPECIFICS: The best treatment for neuritis is to make sure the patient gets optimum nutrition.
SINGLE HERBS: Black Cohosh, Lobelia, Lady Slipper, Skullcap, and Valerian Root.
VITAMINS: B1, B2, B6, B12, Niacin and Pantothenic acid.
MINERALS: A strong Multi-mineral plus Calcium and Magnesium.
TISSUE SALTS: Calc phos, Mag phos, and Silicea.
ALSO: Lecithin, Protein, and Proteolytic Enzymes.
REFERENCES:
Lets Get Well - A. Davis
Nutrition Abstracts - R. Ropert

NIGHT BLINDNESS ...
HERBAL COMBINATION:
(Herbal Eyebright Formula)
PHYSIOLOGIC ACTION:
Extremely valuable in strengthening and healing the eyes. Aids the body in healing lesions and eye injuries.
Warning: If symptoms persist discontinue use.
SINGLE HERBS: Bilberry and Eyebright.
VITAMINS: A Multi-vitamin complex plus A, B1, B2, B3, B5, B6, C, D, and E.
MINERALS: Calcium, Copper, Manganese, Magnesium, Potassium, Selenium, and Zinc.
ESSENTIAL OILS: Lavender and Orange.

ALSO: Gyncydo and Protein.
REFERENCES:
Herbally Yours - P. Royal
The Complete Natural Health Encyclopedia - David Nyholt

NOCTURIA.....

HERBAL COMBINATION: (KB)
PHYSIOLOGIC ACTION: Valuable in healing and strengthening the kidneys, bladder, and genitourinary area.
SINGLE HERBS: Alfalfa, Barberry Root, Catnip, Dandelion, Fennel, Ginger Root, Goldenrod, Horsetail, Uva Vrsi, and Wild Yam.
VITAMINS: A, B Complex, C, D, E, and Choline.
MINERALS: Calcium, Magnesium, and Potassium.
ESSENTIAL OILS: Tea Tree Oil.
FLOWER REMEDIES: Hornbeam, Impatiens, Mimulus, and Mustard.
ALSO: Digestive Enzymes, Lecithin, and 3 Way Herb Teas.
REFERENCES:
Natural Treatments and Remedies - Global Health

OBESITY.....

HERBAL COMBINATIONS:
(SKC) or (Herbal Slim)
PHYSIOLOGIC ACTION: This effective formula cleanses the bowels and eliminates excess water. Helps control appetite, dissolves excess fat, reduces tension, stress and anxiety associated with dieting.
SINGLE HERBS: Chickweed, Hawthorn Berries, Kelp, Licorice Root, Papaya Leaves, and Saffron.
VITAMINS: B2, B5, B6, B12, B complex, C, E, Choline, Folic Acid, Inositol, and Lecithin.
MINERALS: Calcium, Magnesium, and Phosphorus.
ESSENTIAL OILS: Bergamot, Fennel, and Patchouli.

FLOWER REMEDIES: Larch and Honeysuckle.
ALSO: Yu-ccan herbal drink, Protein, and Unsaturated fatty acids.
REFERENCES:
Nutrition Almanac - J. Kirschmann
The Athletes Bible - David Nyholt
The Fitness Formula - Steve Sokol

ORAL CANCER.....
Refer to *Cancer* Page 21

ORAL THRUSH.....

HERBAL COMBINATION:
(Cantrol)
PHYSIOLOGIC ACTION: Excellent well balanced formulas for control and eventual elimination of yeast.
SINGLE HERBS: Black Walnut, Caprinex, Garlic, and Pau d'Arco.
VITAMINS: A, C, E, and Biotin.
ESSENTIAL OILS: Tea Tree Oil.
FLOWER REMEDIES: Holly, Impatiens, and White Chestnut.
TISSUE SALTS: Silicea.
ALSO: Primrose oil, Protein, and Primadophilus.
REFERENCES:
Natural Treatments and Remedies - Global Health
The Complete Natural Health Encyclopedia - David Nyholt.

OSTEOARTHRITIS.....

HERBAL COMBINATION:
(Rheum- Aid) (Yucca - AR)
PHYSIOLOGIC ACTION: Helps the body reduce or eliminate swelling and inflammation in the joints and connective tissue.
SINGLE HERBS: Alfalfa, Black Cohash, Burdock, Cayenne, Celery Seed, Chaparral, Devil's Claw, Valerian Root, and Yucca.

VITAMINS: Niacin, B5, B6, B12, B Complex, C, D, E, F, and P.
MINERALS: A strong Multi-Mineral Plus Calcium, and Magnesium.
ESSENTIAL OILS: Geranium, Lavender, and Wintergreen.
FLOWER REMEDIES: Aspen and Willow.
ALSO: Cod Liver Oil, Green Magma, Aqua Life, Seatone, and Bromelain.
REFERENCES:
Herbally Yours - P. Royal
Natural Treatments and Remedies - Global Health
The Complete Natural Health Encyclopedia - David Nyholt

OSTEOPOROSIS .....
SINGLE HERBS: Feverfew, Horsetail, and Oatstraw.
VITAMINS: B12, C, D, and E.
MINERALS: Calcium, Copper, Fluoride, Magnesium, and Phosphorus..
FLOWER REMEDIES: Hornbeam.
ALSO: L-Arginine, L-Lysine, Protein, Multidigestive Enzymes with Betaine Hydrochloride, and Proteolytic Enzymes.
REFERENCES:
Natural Treatments and Remedies - Global Health
The Complete Natural Health Encyclopedia - David Nyholt

PAIN .....
(Headaches - Tension)
HERBAL COMBINATION: (A-P)
PHYSIOLOGIC ACTION: Helps relieve pain in any part of the body. A natural way to ease chronic pain, headaches, childbirth after-pains, aching teeth, nervous tension, spasms and intestinal gas.
SINGLE HERBS: Pau d'Arco.
MINERALS: Calcium.

ESSENTIAL OILS: Bergamot, Birch, Eucalyptus, and Peppermint.
FLOWER REMEDIES: Take Bachs Rescue Remedy.
TISSUE SALTS: Mag phos.
ALSO: DLPA (amino acid), Lobelia, and Pau d'Arco.
REFERENCES:
Diets to Help Headaches - Nightingale
The Athletes Bible – David Nyholt

PANCREATITIS .....
HERBAL COMBINATION: (PC)
PHYSIOLOGIC ACTION: Helps eliminate mucus and sedimentation, arrest infection, and stimulate and restore the natural functions of the pancreas. Also used for blood-sugar problems and healing the spleen.
SINGLE HERBS: Dandelion, Golden Seal, Juniper Berries, and Uva Ursi.
VITAMINS: A, B complex, C, E, Choline, and Inositol.
MINERALS: Chromium, Potassium and Zinc.
ESSENTIAL OILS: Lavender, Lemon, Niaouli, and Orange.
FLOWER REMEDIES: Mimulus and Red Chestnut.
ALSO: Coenzyme Q10, Germanium, lecithin, Proteolytic Enzymes, and Raw Pancreas Concentrate.
REFERENCES:
Glandular Extracts - Donsbach
How to Get Well - P. Airola

PARASITES .....
HERBAL COMBINATIONS: (Para-X) (Para-VF)
PHYSIOLOGIC ACTION: Useful in destroying and eliminating parasites, such as worms. Also helps relieve many kinds of skin problems. The Para-VF is liquid and is

53

useful for children and the elderly who cannot swallow capsules.

Warning: Do not use during pregnancy.

SINGLE HERBS: Black Walnut, Garlic, Pumpkin Seeds, Sage, Swedish Bitters and Wormwood.

VITAMINS: Folic Acid.

TISSUE SALTS: Kali mur, Mag phos, and Mat phos.

CHILDREN: Camomile tea, or raisins soaked in Senna tea for older children may be helpful.

REFERENCES:
The Miracle of Garlic – P..Airola
Herbally Yours - P. Royal

PARKINSON'S DISEASE .....

SPECIFICS: A low protein diet of raw organic foods is best for patients with Parkinson's Disease.

SINGLE HERBS: Ginseng, Damiana, and Cayenne

VITAMINS: B complex, plus B2, B6, C, and E.

MINERALS: Calcium Lactate, and Magnesium.

FLOWER REMEDIES: Combine Beech, Holy, Impatiens, and White Chestnut.

ALSO: Brewer's yeast, Lecithin, Multi-digestive Enzymes, L-Glutamic Acid, and L-Tyrosine.

REFERENCES:
New Breed of Doctor - A. Nittler
Ann. Rev. Med. 22: 305 - G. Cotzais

PEPTIC ULCERS .....

HERBAL COMBINATION:
(Myrrh- Gold Seal Plus)

SINGLE HERBS: Golden Seal, Myrrh, Pau d' Arco, Red Raspberry, Slippery Elm Bark, Valerian, and White Oak Bark.

VITAMINS: A, B2, B5, B6, B12, B Complex, C, D, E, P, Choline, and Folic Acid.

MINERALS: Calcium, Magnesium, and Zinc.

ESSENTIAL OILS: Lavender and Orange.

FLOWER REMEDIES: Combine Holly, Impatiens, Larcg, and White Chestnut.

ALSO: Acidophilus, Adrenal Glandular Extract, Bioflavonoids, Bromelain, and Glutamine.

REFERENCES:
Natural Treatments and Remedies - Global Health
The Complete Natural Health Encyclopedia - David Nyholt

PHLEBITIS .....

HERBAL COMBINATIONS: (H Formula) (Garlicin HC)

PHYSIOLOGIC ACTION: The herbs in these combinations are known to strengthen and support the cardiovascular system. Supplementing the body with niacin (B3), may be useful to help prevent clot formation. Vitamin C can help strengthen the blood vessel walls. Some research indicates that vitamin E may dilate the blood vessels, thus discouraging the formation of varicose veins and phlebitis.

SINGLE HERBS: Ginkgo, Horse Chestnut and Yarrow.

VITAMINS: B complex, B3, C, and E.

MINERALS: A multi-mineral Complex.

ESSENTIAL OILS: Camphor, Cumin, Hyssop, and Rosemary.

FLOWER REMEDIES: Holly and Hornbeam.

REFERENCES:
Nutrition Almanac - J. Kirschmann

PINK EYE.....
SINGLE HERBS: Hot compresses made from Chamomile or Fennel tea may be helpful for irritation.
VITAMINS: A, B2, B6, B Complex, Niacin, C, and D.
MINERALS: Calcium, Magnesium, Phosphorus, and Zinc.
FLOWER REMEDIES: Impatiens.
REFERENCES:
Nutrition Almanac - J. Kirschmann
Herbally Yours - P. Royal
The Complete Natural Health Encyclopedia - David Nyholt
Natural Treatments and Remedies - Global Health

PINWORMS.....
Refer to *Parasites* Page 53

PLEURISY.....
SINGLE HERBS: Cordyceps, Corn Silk, Sage, and Pine Bark.
VITAMINS: A and C.
MINERALS: A high potency Multi-mineral.
ESSENTIAL OILS: Bergamot, Birch, Calendula, and Chamomile.
FLOWER REMEDIES: Mustard, Olive, and Sweet Chestnut.
TISSUE SALTS: Calc phos and Ferr phos.
ALSO: Bromelain.
REFERENCES:
The Complete Natural Health Encyclopedia - David Nyholt.

PNEUMONIA.....
HERBAL COMBINATIONS:
(Garlicin CF) (Herbal Influenza)
SINGLE HERBS: Boneset, Comfrey, EchinaGuard, Eucalyptus, Fenugreek, Licorice, and Mullein.
VITAMINS: A, B complex, Ester C with Bioflavonoids, E, K, and P.
MINERALS: Zinc.

ESSENTIAL OILS: Camphor, Eucalyptus, and Fir.
FLOWER REMEDIES: Take Bachs Rescue Remedy.
TISSUE SALTS: Ferr phos and Kali mur.
REFERENCES:
Back to Eden - J. Kloss
Herbally Yours - P. Royal
Nutrition Almanac - J. Kirschmann

POOR CIRCULATION..
Refer to *Circulation* Page 23

PREMATURE AGING..
Refer to *Aging* Page 10

PREMENSTRUAL SYNDROME (P.M.S.).....
Refer to *Menstruation* Page 48

PRE-NATAL PREPARATION.....
HERBAL COMBINATION:
(Healthy Greens)
PHYSIOLOGIC ACTION: A complete combination of vitamins and minerals containing digestive aids to ensure proper assimilation.
SINGLE HERBS: Blessed Thistle, Chamomile, Chlorella, Lobelia, and Red Raspberry,
VITAMINS: A, B Complex, B12, C, D, and E.
MINERALS: Multi-mineral Complex plus Calcium, Magnesium, and Phosphorus.
ALSO: Bone Meal, Brewer's Yeast, and Kelp.
REFERENCES:
Herbally Yours - P. Royal
Pregnancy - Donsbach
Every Woman's Book - P. Airola

PROLAPSUS.....
HERBAL COMBINATION:
(Yellow dock Combination)

55

PHYSIOLOGIC ACTION: Helps revitalize a prolapsed uterus, kidneys, and bowel, it also has been proven effective for hemorrhoids, colitis, and as a good purifier.
SINGLE HERBS: Black Walnut, Calendula, Marshmallow Root, Mullein, White Oak Bark, and Yellow Dock.
REFERENCES:
Health Through God's Pharmacy - M. Treben
Every Woman's Book - P. Airola

PROSTATE CANCER...
Refer to *Cancer* Page 21

PROSTATE - KIDNEY
(DISORDERS).....
HERBAL COMBINATION: (PR)
PHYSIOLOGIC ACTION: This formula helps cleanse sedimentation and arrest infection in the prostate and dissolve kidney stones to restore these glands to the natural functions.
SINGLE HERBS: Cayenne, Bee Pollen, Golden Seal, Juniper Berries, Siberian Ginseng, and Uva Ursi.
ALSO: ProActive is an herbal extract of Saw Palmetto.
VITAMINS: A, B complex, B6, C, E, and F.
MINERALS: Calcium, Magnesium, and Zinc.
ESSENTIAL OILS: Tea Tree Oil.
FLOWER REMEDIES: Hornbean, Impatiens, Mimulus, and Mustard.
TISSUE SALTS: Ferr phos, Kali phos, and Kali Mur.
PROSTATE SPECIFICS: Also regularity in sexual habit, lots of walking and other exercise.
REFERENCES:
Health Through God's Pharmacy - M. Treben
Kidney Disorders - H. Clements

56

PSORIASIS.....
HERBAL COMBINATIONS:
(AKN) (Evening Primrose)
(Thisilyn)
PHYSIOLOGIC ACTION: The above herbs taken in combination has a dramatic effect on this disorder.
SINGLE HERBS: Chickweed, Dandelion, Goldenseal, Lobelia, Skullcap, St. Johns Wort, and Yellow Dock.
VITAMINS: A, B complex, C, D, E, Folic Acid, and Lecithin.
MINERALS: Calcium, Magnesium, Sulfur Ointment, and Zinc.
ESSENTIAL OILS: Calendula, Chamomile, Lavender, and Rose.
FLOWER REMEDIES: Chicory, Impatiens, and Red Chestnut.
TISSUE SALTS: Calc sulph and Kali sulph.
ALSO: Diet and stress are key factors in this skin disorder. Certain allergen foods need to be completely avoided. Dairy and wheat are especially harmful in many instances. Fat should be kept to a minimum.
REFERENCES:
How to Get Well - P. Airola
Nutrition Almanac - Kirschmann
Indian Herbology - A. Hutchens

PYORRHEA.....
SINGLE HERBS: Golden Seal, and Myrrh.
PHYSIOLOGIC ACTION: Use these powders on tooth brush, or make a tea, which is one teaspoon of each the Golden Seal and Myrrh, in one pint of boiling water. Steep. Rinse mouth and gargle with it freely, also, brush gums with tea.
VITAMINS: A, B1, B2, B6, B12, C, D, and E. Rub the gums morning and evening with vitamin E.

MINERALS: Calcium, Magnesium, and Zinc.
ESSENTIAL OILS: Myrrh, Tea tree, and Thyme.
REFERENCES:
Back to Eden - J. Kloss
Nutrition Almanac - Kirschmann

QUINSY .....
HERBAL COMBINATION: (IF) (IGL)
PHYSIOLOGIC ACTION:
Effective formulas that help cleanse toxins, combat infections, and heal the lymphatic system.
SINGLE HERBS: Bayberry Root, EchinaGuard, Enchinacea, Ginger Root, and Pau d' Arco.
VITAMINS: A complete multi-complex.
ALSO: Canaid herbal drink.
REFERENCES:
Nutrition Almanac - Kirschmann
Natural Treatments & Remedies
The Complete Natural Health Encyclopedia - David Nyholt

RHEUMATIC FEVER ..
SINGLE HERBS: Birch Leaves, Catnip, Dandelion, Fenugreek, Garlic, Lobelia, Thyme, and Pau d' Arco.
VITAMINS: A complete multi-complex plus A, B2, B6, C, D, and E.
MINERALS: Zinc
ESSENTIAL OILS: Bergamot, Geranium, Thyme, and Violet.
FLOWER REMEDIES: Gorse and Sweet chestnut.
ALSO: Canaid herbal drink, Bioflav- onoids, Coenzyme Q10, and Germanium.
REFERENCES:
Back to Eden - J. Kloss
Indian Herbalogy of North America - A. R. Hutchens

The Complete Natural Health Encyclopedia - David Nyholt

RHEUMATISM .....
HERBAL COMBINATIONS:
(Yucca-AR) or (Rheum-Aid)
PHYSIOLOGIC ACTION: Excellent formulas for relieving symptoms associated with bursitis, calcification, gout, rheumatoid arthritis, rheumatism and osteoarthritis. It helps to reduce or eliminate swellings inflammation in joints, connective tissues and relieves stiffness and pain.
SINGLE HERBS: Alfalfa, Chaparral, Cayenne, Fennel, Garlic, Pau d'Arco, Red Clover, Red Raspberry and Yucca.
VITAMINS: B complex, B5, B15, C, and E.
MINERALS: Calcium, Magnesium phosphorus, Potassium, and Zinc.
ESSENTIAL OILS: Lavender, Pine, and Rosemary.
FLOWER REMEDIES: Aspen and Willow.
ALSO: Yu-ccan herbal drink Digestive Enzymes, and Hydrochloric Acid.
REFERENCES:
Folk Medicine - Crest
Back to Eden - J. Kloss
How to Get Well - P. Airola

RINGING IN EARS .....
Refer to *Tinnitus* Page 63

RINGWORM .....
HERBAL COMBINATION: (Black Walnut Extract)
SINGLE HERBS: Black Walnut, Golden Seal, Pau d'Arco. Rub skin with black walnut extract, Apple Cider Vinegar or Castor Oil, several times a day.
VITAMINS: A, B Complex, and C.
MINERALS: Zinc.

ESSENTIAL OILS: Tea Tree Oil.
TISSUE SALTS: Silicea.
ALSO: Germanium and Unsaturated Fatty Acids.
REFERENCES:
How to Get Well - P. Airola
Herbally Yours - P. Royal

ROUNDWORMS.....

HERBAL COMBINATION: (Para-X) (Para-VF)
PHYSIOLOGIC ACTION: Para-X is useful in destroying and eliminating parasites. Para-VF is a liquid and is used for children and the elderly who cannot swallow capsules.
SINGLE HERBS: Black Walnut, Garlic, Pumpkin Seeds, and Wormwood.
VITAMINS: Folic Acid.
ESSENTIAL OILS: Bergamot, Hyssop, Juniper, and Tarragon.
FLOWER REMEDIES: Combine Aspen, Gorse, and Willow.
ALSO: Swedish Bitters.
REFERENCES:
Nutrition Almanac - J. Kirschmann
Natural Treatments and Remedies -Global Health
The Complete Natural Health Encyclopedia - David Nyholt

SALMONELLA.....
Refer to *Food Poisoning* Page 34

SCIATICA.....

HOMEOPATHIC REMEDY:
(Injury and Backache Formula)
PHYSIOLOGIC ACTION: For natural symptomatic relief of pain and discomfort.
SINGLE HERBS: Pau d' Arco.
VITAMINS: B1, B12, B Complex, D, and E.
MINERALS: Multi-mineral.
ESSENTIAL OILS: Ginger, Lavender, Marjoram, and Rosemary.

FLOWER REMEDIES: Take Bachs Rescue Remedy.
TISSUE SALTS: Ferr phos and Kali phos.
REFERENCES:
Natural Treatments and Remedies
The Complete Natural Health Encyclopedia - David Nyholt

SCURVY.....

SINGLE HERBS: Kelp and Yucca.
VITAMINS: A, B Complex, C, and D.
MINERALS: Calcium, Iron, and Magnesium.
ALSO: Yu-ccan herbal drink and Protein.
REFERENCES:
Nutrition Almanac - J. Kirschmann
Natural Treatments and Remedies - Global Health
The Complete Natural Health Encyclopedia - David Nyholt

SKIN CANCER.....
Refer to *Cancer* Page 21

SEIZURES.....
Refer to *Epilepsy* Page 31

SENILITY.....

HERBAL COMBINATIONS:
(SEN) or (Remem)
PHYSIOLOGIC ACTION: An excellent combination to nourish the brain cells, tissues and improves their ability to perform mental functions.
SINGLE HERBS: Dandelion, Ginkgo, Ginseng, Gotu Kola, Licorice, and Yellow Dock.
VITAMINS: A, B3, B complex, C, and E.
MINERALS: Choline and Zinc.
ESSENTIAL OILS: Basil, Lemon, Rosemary, and Verbena.

FLOWER REMEDIES: Clematis.
ALSO: Coenzyme Q10, Geranium, Lecithin, and Protein.
REFERENCES:
Antioxidants - Passwater
Herbally Yours - P. Royal

SHINGLES .....
(Herpes Zoster)
PHYSIOLOGIC ACTION: B vitamins are necessary for the proper functioning of the nerves. Vitamins A and C promote healing of skin lesions, and heavy doses of vitamin C can limit infection of lesions.
VITAMINS: A, B complex, C, and D.
MINERALS: Calcium, and Magnesium
ESSENTIAL OILS: Geranium, Lemon, and Tea Tree Oil.
FLOWER REMEDIES: Gentain and Gorse.
TISSUE SALTS: Ferr phos, Kali phos, and Nat mur.
ALSO: L-Lysine and Protein.
REFERENCES:
Nutrition Almanac - J.Kirschmann
The Complete Natural Health Encyclopedia - David Nyholt.

SHOCK .....
SINGLE HERBS: Nettle, Peppermint, Yellow Dock, and Ginseng.
VITAMINS: B complex and C.
MINERALS: A high potency multi-mineral.
ESSENTIAL OILS: Camphor and Melissa.
FLOWER REMEDIES: Take Bachs Rescue Remedy.
ALSO: Protein and L-Tryptophan.
REFERENCES:
The Complete Natural Health Encyclopedia - David Nyholt.

SINUS PROBLEMS .....
HERBAL COMBINATIONS:
(HAS) (Zand Decongest Herbal Formula) (Garlicin CF)
SINGLE HERBS: Comfrey, Elderberry, Eyebright, Fenugreek, and Golden Seal.
VITAMINS: A, B complex, B5, C, and E.
MINERALS: Potassium and Zinc.
ESSENTIAL OILS: Fir, Garlic, Tea Tree, and Thyme.
FLOWER REMEDIES: Gorse and Mustard.
TISSUE SALTS: Kali sulph and Nat mur.
ALSO: Bee Pollen, Coenzyme Q10, Garlic, Germanium, Protein, and Proteolytic Enzymes.
REFERENCES:
Diets to Help Catarrh - A. Moyle

SKIN .....
(Bites, Stings, and Poisons)
HERBAL COMBINATION:
(EchinaGuard).
PHYSIOLOGIC ACTION:
Echinacea was used by the plains Indians to lessen the effects of poisonous bites. EchinaGuard would be very beneficial. Take large doses of vitamin C and Calcium. Use vitamin E topically to reduce pain.
SINGLE HERBS: Echinacea.
VITAMINS: Multi-Vitamin.
MINERALS: Multi-Mineral.
ESSENTIAL OILS: Tea Tree Oil.
REFERENCES:
"How to Get Well"—P. Airola

SKIN .....
SINGLE HERBS: Hautex.
PHYSIOLOGIC ACTION: To work from within to encourage skin se-

cretion, effective for acne, blackheads, pimples, itch and rash.
VITAMINS: A, B complex, E, C, and Rosehips.
ALSO: Efamol, Whey Powder, and Acidophilus

SKIN BLEMISHES.....
HERBAL COMBINATION: AKN.
PHYSIOLOGIC ACTION: Diulaxa tea helps cleanse the bloodstream. Pimples, blackheads, and other superficial skin eruptions, and more serious conditions such as boils, carbuncles, dermatitis, eczema, and pleuritis will be eliminated when the blood has been cleansed.
VITAMINS: A, B2, B3, B5, B6, C, F, P, Biotin, and Paba.
MINERALS: Iron, Silicon, and Sulfur.
ALSO: Whey Powder, and Brewers Yeast.
REFERENCES:
Diets to Help Acne - A. Moyle

SKIN CANCER.....
Refer to *Melanoma* Page 47

SKIN PROBLEMS.....
1. **Dry Skin** — Chamomile, Dandelion, Licorice, Oat Extract, Evening Primrose Oil, Vitamin A, B complex, C, Aloe Vera, Add Herbal oils to bath (Lavender oil is very nice)
2. **Itchy Skin** — Chickweed, Calendula, Elder, Yarrow, vegetable oil daily, apple cider vinegar to bath. X-Itch ointment is also very effective.
3. **Oily Skin** — Vitamin B complex, Liver, and Rosemary.
4. **Scars** — Vitamin E orally and topically.
5. **Stretch marks** — Vitamin E, B complex, B5, C, Aloe Vera, Zinc, and Carnation oil.
6. **Sunburn** — B vitamins, Paba, C, E, Calcium, Zinc, and Aloe Vera.
7. **Wrinkles** — Vitamins A, B complex, E, Zinc, Selenium, and Almond oil.
REFERENCES:
Secrets of Natural Beauty - Castleton
Swedish Beauty Secrets-P. Airola
How to Get Well - P. Airola

SMOKING.....
HERBAL COMBINATIONS: (Milk thistle extract) or (Thisilyn)
PHYSIOLOGIC ACTION: These herbal combinations decrease the desire for tobacco and protect the liver from the negative effects of smoking. Vitamins and minerals should be taken to rebuild the nutritional system after a juice fast. The juice fast cleanses the accumulated poisons from the body, thus eliminating the physiological dependence.
Note: Tobacco, alcohol, caffeine and other drug "cravings" are brought about by a physiological body dependence on the poison which develops during prolonged use. The addicts blood poison level must remain at a certain level at all times. As the poison level drops, there is a "desire" to take in more of the drug, to bring the level back again
SINGLE HERBS: Catnip, Chaparral, Hops, Licorice, Lobelia, Skullcap, Slippery Elm, and Valerian.
VITAMINS AND MINERALS: All.
ESSENTIAL OILS: Chamomile, Grapefruit, Juniper, and Lavender.
FLOWER REMEDIES: Combine Holly, Impatiens, Larch, Olive, and Sweat Chestnut.

AMINO ACIDS: L-Cysteine, L-Cystine, and L- Methionine.
ALSO: Fasting: drink juice only.
REFERENCES:
How to Get Well - P.Airola
Drugs and Beyond - David Nyholt
The Complete Natural Health Encyclopedia - David Nyholt.
Vitamin Bible - E. Mindell
Good News for Smokers -Donsbach

SNORING .....

HERBAL COMBINATION: (HAS) (Sinustop) and (Fenu-Thyme)
PHYSIOLOGIC ACTION: These combinations promote sinus drainage and shrink swollen membranes.
SINGLE HERBS: Lobelia, Mullen, Red Clover, and Rose Hips.
VITAMINS: A multi-vitamin.
MINERALS: A multi-mineral plus extra Calcium and Magnesium.
ESSENTIAL OILS: Eucalyptus, Fir, Tea Tree, and Thyme.
FLOWER REMEDIES: Gorse and Mustard.
TISSUE SALTS: ..
ALSO: Digestive-enzymes.
REFERENCES:
The Complete Natural Health Encyclopedia - David Nyholt.

SORE THROAT .....

HERBAL COMBINATION: (IF) (IGL).
PHYSIOLOGIC ACTION: Useful formulas to combat and heal infections caused by cigarette smoke, environmental pollutants, and overuse of voice.
SINGLE HERBS: Bayberry Root, Echinacea, Ginger, and Pau d Arco.
VITAMINS: A, B complex, B3, B6, C, and E.
MINERALS: A Complete multi-mineral.

ESSENTIAL OILS: Bergamot, Geranium, Thyme, and Violet.
FLOWER REMEDIES: Gorse and Sweet Chestnut.
ALSO: Canaid herbal drink.
REFERENCES:
Natural Treatments and Remedies - Global Health
The Complete Natural Health Encyclopedia - David Nyholt

SPASTIC COLON .....
Refer to *Colitis* Page 25

SPIDER VEINS .....
Refer to *Varicose Veins* Page 65

STRESS .....
HERBAL COMBINATIONS:
(Calm aid) (Ex stress) (Kalmin extract)
PHYSIOLOGIC ACTION: Special formulas for insomnia and stress related conditions. Relieve nervous tension, rebuilds nerve sheaths. Soothing and calming effect on the whole nervous system.
SINGLE HERBS: Black Cohosh Root, Cayenne, Lady's Slipper, Skullcap, and Valerian Root.
VITAMINS: A, all B's, C, D, E, Paba, Folic Acid, & Choline.
MINERALS: Calcium, Chromium, Copper, Iron, Selenium, and Zinc.
ESSENTIAL OILS: Chamomile, Eucalyptus, Geranium, Lavender, and Pine.
FLOWER REMEDIES: Take Bachs Rescue Remedy and White Chestnut.
ALSO: L-Tyrosine and Protein.
REFERENCES:
Stress - Donsbach
The Athletes Bible – David Nyholt
The Fitness Formula - S. Sokol
Indian Herbology of N America - A. Hutchens

STRETCH MARKS.....

Refer to *Skin Problems* Page 60

STROKE.....

HERBAL COMBINATION:
(Garlicin HC)
PHYSIOLOGIC ACTION: A combination of herbs which supports the cardiovascular system. Helps to strengthen the heart, while building and cleansing the arteries and veins.
SINGLE HERBS: Cayenne, Comfrey, Evening Primrose Oil, Fish Oil, Garlic, Golden Seal, and Rose Hips.
VITAMINS: B Complex, C, E, Niacin, Inositol, and Choline.
MINERALS: A Multi-mineral, plus Calcium, and Magnesium.
FLOWER REMEDIES: Take Bachs Rescue Remedy.
ALSO: Cold pressed vegetable oils..
REFERENCES:
Natural Treatments & Remedies
The Complete Natural Health Encyclopedia - David Nyholt

SUNBURN.....

Refer to *Skin Problems* Page 60

SUNSTROKE.....

SINGLE HERBS: Linden and Passionflower.
ESSENTIAL OILS: Lavender, Peppermint, and Rose.
FLOWER REMEDIES: Take Bachs Rescue Remedy.
TISSUE SALTS: Ferr phos.
ALSO: Acidophilus, Green drink supplements, and Salt.
REFERENCES:
The Complete Natural Health Encyclopedia - David Nyholt

SYPHILIS.....

SINGLE HERBS: Echinacea, Golden Seal, Pau d' Arco, Red Clover, and Suma.
VITAMINS: A, B complex, and K.
MINERALS: Zinc.
ESSENTIAL OILS: Neroli and Niaouli.
FLOWER REMEDIES: Combine Holly, Hornbeam, Impatiens, and White Chestnut.
TISSUE SALTS: Ferr phos, Kali phos, and Nat mur.
ALSO: Acidophilus, Coenzyme Q10, Germanium, and Protein.
REFERENCES:
The Complete Natural Health Encyclopedia - David Nyholt

TAPEWORMS.....

Refer to *Worms* Page 67

TEETH AND GUMS....

SINGLE HERBS: Chamomile, Echinacea, Lobelia, Myrrh Gum, and White Oak Bark.
VITAMINS: A, B complex, C, D, P, Folic Acid.
MINERALS: Calcium, Magnesium, Phosphorus, and Silicon.
ALSO: Protein and Unsaturated Fatty Acids.
1. Toothache — Primrose oil or oil of cloves.
2. Stained or yellow teeth — brush with fresh strawberries.
REFERENCES:
Nutrition Almanac - J. Kirschmann
Herbally Yours - P. Royal
How to Get Well - P. Airola

TEETH GRINDING.....

SINGLE HERBS: Chamomile, and Skullcap.
VITAMINS: Multi vit., B complex. Take tablets before bed for best results.
ESSENTIAL OILS: Almond, Bergamot, Geranium, and Lavender.

FLOWER REMEDIES: Combine Aspen, Elm, and Red Chestnut.
ALSO: Bonemeal or other Calcium supplement.
REFERENCES:
How to Get Well - P. Airola
Vitamin Bible - E. Mindell

TEETHING .....
SINGLE HERBS: Lobelia Extract, Aloe Vera Gel, or Peppermint Oil can be rubbed on the gums.
TISSUE SALTS: combination "R."
ESSENTIAL OILS: Add Chamomile and Lavender to bath, to calm a distressed baby.
FLOWER REMEDIES: Walnut.
TISSUE SALTS: Silicea.
ALSO: Teething Tablets from Hylands.
REFERENCES:
Herbally Yours - P. Royal

TENSION .....
Refer to *Stress* Page 61

TESTICULAR CANCER .
Refer to *Cancer* Page 21

THROAT CANCER .....
Refer to *Cancer* Page 21

THYROID .....
HERBAL COMBINATION: (T.)
PHYSIOLOGIC ACTION: Rich in natural vitamins and minerals, this excellent formula helps revitalize and promote healing of the thyroid glands thus restoring metabolism balance. Helps the body store up needed vitality and energy.
SINGLE HERBS: Black Walnut, Irish Moss, Kelp, Mullein, and Parsley.
VITAMINS: B1, B5, C, D, E, F.
MINERALS: Chlorine, Iodine, Potassium, and Zinc.

ESSENTIAL OILS: Lemon and Palmarosa.
ALSO: Thyroid glandular
REFERENCES:
Herbally Yours - P. Royal
Health Through God's Pharmacy - M. Treben

TINNITUS .....
HERBAL COMBINATION: (H Formula) (Ginkgold)
PHYSIOLOGIC ACTION: Improves circulation and pulse rate, giving a warming and calming sensation to the ears.
SINGLE HERBS: Cayenne, Black Cohosh, Bayberry, Butchers Broom, Ginkgo, and Yarrow.
VITAMINS: A, B Complex, B3, B6, C, and E.
MINERALS: Calcium, Magnesium, Manganese, and Potassium.
ESSENTIAL OILS: Camphor, Cumin, Pine, and Rosemary.
FLOWER REMEDIES: Beech and Impatiens.
TISSUE SALTS: Ferr phos, Kali phos, and Mag phos.
ALSO: Bio-Strath, Coenzyme Q10, and Lecithin.
REFERENCES:
Nutrition Almanac - J. Kirschmann
Natural Treatments and Remedies - Global Health
The Complete Natural Health Encyclopedia - David Nyholt
How to Get Well - P. Airola
Indian Herbology of N America - A. Hutchens

TIREDNESS .....
Refer to *Fatigue General* Page 33

TONSILITIS .....
HERBAL COMBINATIONS: (IF) (IGL)
PHYSIOLOGIC ACTION: Effective formulas that helps cleanse

toxins, combat infections, and reduce infection. Especially effective for healing lymphatic system.

SINGLE HERBS: Bayberry Root, Echina Guard, Echinacea, Ginger Root, and Pau d' Arco.
VITAMINS AND MINERALS: A complete one a day multi complex.
ESSENTIAL OILS: Bergamot, Geranium, Thyme, and Violet.
FLOWER REMEDIES: Gorse and Sweet Chestnut.
TISSUE SALTS: Kali mur.
ALSO: Canaid herbal drink.

TOOTHACHE.....
Refer to *Teeth & Gums* Page 62

TRENCH MOUTH.....
Refer to *Gingivitis* Page 35

TUMORS (BENIGN)...
SINGLE HERBS: Dandelion, Kelp, Pau d'Arco, and Red Clover.
VITAMINS: A, B5, B6, B Complex, C, and E.
MINERALS: A high potency Multimineral.
ESSENTIAL OILS: Cypress and Rose.
FLOWER REMEDIES: Take Bachs Rescue Remedy as needed.
TISSUE SALTS: Kali phos and Mag phos.
ALSO: Coenzyme Q10, Germanium, Lecithin, Proteolytic Enzymes, and Sheep Sorrel is an excellent poultice for external tumors.
REFERENCES:
Nutrition Almanac - J. Kirschmann
Natural Treatments and Remedies - Global Health
The Complete Natural Health Encyclopedia - David Nyholt

ULCERS - (SKIN).....
HERBAL COMBINATION: (Myrrh – Golden seal)
PHYSIOLOGIC ACTION: Ingredients needed by the body to heal ulcers, cuts, wounds, bruises, sprains and burns. Good as a poultice for external wounds.
VITAMINS: Folic Acid, Panothenic Acid, C, and E.
MINERALS: A Multi-mineral complex.
ALSO: Aloe Vera
Skin ulcers that do not heal — Vitamin E, topical application of comfrey root and/or tea leaf. Dress with a paste made of raw garlic on gauze for 8-10 hours. Take Vitamin C, A, zinc and Calcium orally.
REFERENCES:
The Aloe Vera Handbook - M. Skousen
How to Get Well - P. Airola

ULCERS (STOMACH)..
HERBAL COMBINATION: (Myrrh – Gold Seal Plus)
SINGLE HERBS: Cayenne (stomach ulcers only), Golden Seal, Myrrh, Pau d'Arco, Red Raspberry, Slippery Elm Bark, Valerian, and White Oak Bark.
VITAMINS: A, B complex, B2, B5, B6, B12, C, D, E, P, Choline, and Folic acid.
MINERALS: Calcium, Manganese, and Zinc,
ESSENTIAL OILS: Lavender and Orange.
FLOWER REMEDIES: Combine Holly, Impatiens, and White Chestnut.
TISSUE SALTS: Kali phos, Kali mur, and Nat phos.
ALSO: Acidophilus, Chlorophyll, Raw Cabbage, Potato juice, Goat's

milk, Brewer's yeast, Aloe Vera, and Halibut oil.
Refer to "Digestive Disorders" in this manual.
REFERENCES:
Nutrition Almanac - J. Kirschmann
How to Get Well - P. Airola
Natural Treatments and Remedies - Global Health

URINARY TRACT CANCER.....
Refer to *Cancer* Page 21

VAGINAL PROBLEMS.
(GYNECOLOGICAL PROBLEMS)
HERBAL COMBINATION: (Fem-Mend)
PHYSIOLOGIC ACTION:
Menstrual regulator, tonic for genito-urinary system. Helpful for severe menstrual discomforts. Acts as an aid in rebuilding a malfunctioning reproductive system (Uterus, ovaries, fallopian tubes, etc.)
SINGLE HERBS: Aloe Vera, Blessed Thistle, Comfrey Root, Garlic, Ginger, Golden Seal Root, Red Raspberry, Slippery Elm Bark, Uva Ursi, and Yellow Dock Root,
VITAMINS: A, B complex, C, and E.
MINERALS: A Multi-mineral complex.

VAGINITIS.....
HOMEOPATHIC FORMULA:
(Vaginitis formula)
PHYSIOLOGIC ACTION: For natural relief of minor vaginal burning and itching.
SINGLE HERBS: Garlic and Pau d'Arco.
VITAMINS: A, B Complex, B6, C, and D.

MINERALS: Calcium and Magnesium.
ESSENTIAL OILS: Lavender and Tea Tree Oil.
TISSUE SALTS: Nat phos and Nat mur.
ALSO: Acidophilus, Protein, and Unsaturated fatty acids.
REFERENCES:
Natural Treatments & Remedies
The Complete Natural Health Encyclopedia - David Nyholt

VARICOSE VEINS.....
PHYSIOLOGIC ACTION: Age, lack of exercise and chronic constipation are contributing factors to varicose veins. B and C vitamins are necessary for the maintenance of strong blood vessels. Research has indicated vitamin E improves circulation by dilating blood vessels.
SINGLE HERBS: Butchers Broom, Hawthorn, Horse Chestnut, Marigold, Mistletoe, Witch Hazel, White Oak Bark, and Yarrow.
VITAMINS: B complex, C, and E.
MINERALS: Potassium and Zinc.
ESSENTIAL OILS: Geranium, Ginger, Neroli, and Peppermint.
FLOWER REMEDIES: Hornbeam and Rock Water.
TISSUE SALTS: Calc fluor, Ferr phos, and Mag phos
ALSO: Acidophilus, Protein, and Unsaturated Fatty Acids.
REFERENCES:
Nutrition Almanac - J. Kirschmann
Indian Herbology of N America - A. Hutchens
Vitamin Bible - E. Mindell

VERTIGO.....
HERBAL COMBINATIONS:
(Immun Aid) (B&B Extract) and (EchinaGuard)

PHYSIOLOGIC ACTION: Immun-Aid boosts immunity, thereby helping with ear infections. EchinaGuard is a liquid. Echinacea extract is excellent for small children with ear infections. B&B Extract can be placed in the ear or taken internally. It is also used to aid poor equilibrium, dizzinessand nervous conditions.

SINGLE HERBS: Blue Cohosh, Echinacea, Garlic Oil, Garlic, Mullein Oil, Mullein, Skullcap, and St. Johns Wort.

VITAMINS: A, B complex, and C.

MINERALS: Calcium and Zinc.

ESSENTIAL OILS: Marjoram, Rosemary, and Tea Tree oil.

FLOWER REMEDIES: Take Bachs Rescue Remedy.

TISSUE SALTS: Ferr phos, Kali phos, and Silicea.

ALSO: Propolis, and Primadophilus. When combating ear infections, it is imperative to exclude allergen foods from the diet. This is particularly true of all dairy products.

REFERENCES:
Back to Eden - J. Kloss

WARTS - COMMON ....

SPECIFICS: 28000 IU vitamin E oil applied twice a day is an effective treatment.

SINGLE HERBS: Echinacea, Garlic, Golden Seal, and Pau d' Arco.

VITAMINS: — A, B Complex, C, and E(dry form).

MINERALS: Zinc.

ESSENTIAL OILS: Juniper, Lavender, and Rosemary.

TISSUE SALTS: Kali mur.

REFERENCES:
Vitamin Bible -E. Mindel
How to Get Well -P. Airola

WATER RETENTION ...

HERBAL COMBINATIONS: (KB)

PHYSIOLOGIC ACTION: A mild diuretic to rid the body of excessive water.

SINGLE HERBS: Buchu, Cranberry, Dandelion, Juniper, Parsley, and Uva Ursi.

Note: Limited consumption of common table salt

VITAMINS: B6 and C.

MINERALS: Calcium, and Potassium.

Refer to "Edema" in this manual.

REFERENCES:
Herbally Yours - P. Royal
The Fitness Formula - S. Sokol
The Athletes Bible - David Nyholt
Natural Treatments & Remedies

WEIGHT CONTROL ....

HERBAL COMBINATIONS: (SKC) or (Herbal Slim)

PHYSIOLOGIC ACTION: A special, well balanced combination that helps control your appetite, dissolve excess fat, ease stress and anxiety, gently cleanse the bowels, eliminate excess water, and in conjunction with your diet and exercise program, helps you lose weight naturally. Safe and effective.

SINGLE HERBS: Guar Gum, & Konjac Root.

VITAMINS: A, C, and E.

MINERALS: Multi-mineral Complex.

ESSENTIAL OILS: Bergamot, Fennel, and Patchouli.

FLOWER REMEDIES: Combine Honeysuckle and Larch.

ALSO: Super D's tea, Slim tea, Spirulina diet, Bee Pollen, and Grapefruit Plus.

REFERENCES:
Lose Weight Feel Great -J. Yudkin

All New F Plus Diet - A Eyeton
The Athletes Bible – David Nyholt
The Fitness Formula - S. Sokol

WEIGHT GAIN (UNDERWEIGHT) .....

VITAMINS: B complex.
SINGLE HERBS: Bitter herbs such as those found in Swedish Bitters will stimulate appetite.
ALSO: Digestive enzymes, unsaturated fatty acids, and protein.
REFERENCES:
The Athletes Bible – David Nyholt
The Fitness Formula - Steve Sokol

WHOOPING COUGH ...

HERBAL COMBINATION: (A-P)
PHYSIOLOGIC ACTION: A natural way to ease chronic pain associated with nervous tension, spasms and whooping cough.
SINGLE HERBS: Elecampane, Horehound, Kalmin, Mouse Ear, Sundew, Valerian Root, Wild Cherry Bark, and Wild Lettuce.
ESSENTIAL OILS: Chamomile, Eucalyptus, and Lavender.
FLOWER REMEDIES: Take Bachs Rescue Remedy.

WORMS .....

HERBAL COMBINATION: (Para-X) (Para-VF)
PHYSIOLOGIC ACTION: Para-X is useful in destroying and eliminating parasites. Para-VF is a liquid and is used for children and the elderly who cannot swallow capsules.
SINGLE HERBS: Black Walnut, Garlic, Pumpkin Seeds, and Wormwood.
VITAMINS: Folic Acid.
ESSENTIAL OILS: Bergamot, Hyssop, Juniper, Lemon, Tarragon, and Thuja.

FLOWER REMEDIES: Aspen, Gorse, and Willow.
TISSUE SALTS: Kali mur and Nat phos.
ALSO: Swedish Bitters.
REFERENCES:
Nutrition Almanac - J. Kirschmann
Natural Treatments and Remedies - Global Health
The Complete Natural Health Encyclopedia - David Nyholt

WRINKLES .....
Refer to *Skin Problems* Page 60

YEAST INFECTION ....

HERBAL COMBINATIONS: (Garlicin) (Control, caprinex)
PHYSIOLOGIC ACTION: Excellent well balanced formulas for control and eventual elimination of candida overgrowth.
SINGLE HERBS: Black Walnut, Garlic, and Pau d'Arco.
VITAMINS: A, C, E, and Biotin.
ESSENTIAL OILS: Tea Tree Oil.
FLOWER REMEDIES: Combine Holly, Impatiens, and White Chestnut.
TISSUE SALTS: Calc phos, Kali phos, and Silicea.
ALSO: Primrose oil, Protein, and Primadophilus.
REFERENCES:
Natural Treatments and Remedies - Global Health
The Complete Natural Health Encyclopedia - David Nyholt
Drugs and Beyond – David Nyholt
Candida Albicans - L. Chaitow
The Yeast Connection - Crook

VITAMINS — NATURAL OR SYNTHETIC?

It is a Global opinion that vitamins in their natural, balanced state are essential for better assimilation, synergistic action and maximum biological effect. As a rule of thumb — if the source is not given the product is synthetic. There are however, a growing number of natural supplement manufacturers that use synthetic vitamins, but use the words natural and/or organic on their labels, in order to mislead the public. The guide below will help you break through the deliberate labeling confusion used by some companies. Don't be misled, be an expert label reader even in a health food store.

Vitamin   Source Given

Vitamin		Source Given
Vitamin A	**(Natural)**	**Carrot powder, fish oils, or lemon grass.**
Vitamin A	(Synthetic)	Acetate or palmitate.
Vitamin B1	**(Natural)**	**Rice bran or yeast.**
Vitamin B1	(Synthetic)	Thiamine hydrochloride, thiamine chloride, or thiamine mononitrate.
Vitamin B2	**(Natural)**	**Rice bran or yeast**
Vitamin B2	(Synthetic)	Riboflavin.
Vitamin B3	**(Natural)**	**Rice bran or yeast.**
Vitamin B3	(Synthetic)	If source not given.
Vitamin B5	**(Natural)**	**Yeast.**
Vitamin B5	(Synthetic)	Calcium pantothenate.
Vitamin B9	**(Natural)**	**Yeast.**
Vitamin B9	(Synthetic)	Pteroylglutamic acid.
Vitamin B12	**(Natural)**	**Cobalamine, cyanocobalamin, liver or yeast.**
Vitamin B13	**(Natural)**	**Calcium orotate, or orotic acid.**
Vitamin B15	**(Natural)**	**Calcium pangamate.**
Vitamin B17	**(Natural)**	**Apricot, peach or plum pits.**
B Complex	**(Natural)**	**Brewer's yeast, or soy beans.**
B Complex	(Synthetic)	Choline bitartrate, or d-biotin.
Vitamin C	**(Natural)**	**Rose hips, acerola, or citrus fruits.**
Vitamin C	(Synthetic)	Ascorbic acid or source not given.
Vitamin D	**(Natural)**	**Fish oils.**
Vitamin D	(Synthetic)	Calciferol, or irradiated ergosterol.
Vitamin E	**(Natural)**	**D-alpha tocopherol, tocopherol acetate, mixed tocopherols, wheat germ or veg. oils.**
Vitamin E	(Synthetic)	Alpha tocopherol acetate, or dl-alpha. tocopherol, dl-alpha tocopheryl or acetate.
Vitamin F	**(Natural)**	**Linseed oil or vegetable oils.**
Vitamin H	**(Natural)**	**Yeast.**
Vitamin H	(Synthetic)	D-biotin.
Vitamin K	**(Natural)**	**Alfalfa.**
Vitamin K	(Synthetic)	Menadione.
Vitamin P	**(Natural)**	**Citrus bioflavonoids, citrin, hesperidin, or rutin.**
Vitamin T	**(Natural)**	**Sesame seed.**
Vitamin U	**(Natural)**	**Cabbage extract.**

DOSAGES — VITAMINS & MINERALS

Continual debate rages over what is an (adequate) daily intake of vitamins and minerals. The guide below is just that — a guide only. RDA and Margin of Allowances, are based on the needs of an average adult 23 to 50 years of age, with no special health problems.

	US RDA for adult, 23-50**		Margin of Allowance**	
ViITAMINS				
Vitamin A	5,000 IU		5-10 times RDA	
Thiamin (B1)	1.4 mg		200 times RDA	
Riboflavin (B2)	1.6 mg		588 times RDA	
Niacin (B3)	20 mg		50 times RDA	
Pantothenic acid (B5)	10 mg		100 times RDA	
Pyridoxine (B6)	2 mg		900 times RDA	
Folic acid (B9)	4 mcg		1000 times RDA	
Cobalamin (B12)	6 mcg		n/a	
Orotic acid (B13)	n/a		n/a	
Calc. Pangamate (B15)	(50 mg)	***	(100 mg)	****
Laetrile (B17)	n/a		n/a	
Vitamin C	60 mg		33-83 times RDA	
Vitamin D	400 IU		2.5-5 times RDA	
Vitamin E	10 mg		40 times RDA	
Vitamin F	n/a		n/a	
Vitamin (biotin) H	3 mcg		167 times RDA	
Vitamin K	70 mcg	***	(250 mcg)	****
MINERALS				
Calcium	1000 mg		10 times RDA	
Chlorine	500 mg		(1500 mg)	****
Chromium	(50 mcg)	***	n/a	
Cobalt	(6 mcg)	***	n/a	
Copper	2 mg		5.5 times RDA	
Fluorine	(1 mg)	***	(1.5-4 mg)	****
Iodine	150 mcg		13 times RDA	
Iron	10 mg males		5.5 times RDA	
Iron	18 mg females		5.5 times RDA	
Lithium	n/a		n/a	
Magnesium	400 mg		15 times RDA	
Manganese	2.5-5 mg		n/a	
Molybdenum	(150 mcg)	***	(500 mcg)	****
Phosphorus	1000 mg		10 times RDA	
Potassium	2000 to 2500 mg		n/a	
Selenium	(50 mcg)	***	(150 mcg)	****
Silicon	n/a		n/a	
Sodium	200 to 600 mg		(2 grams)	****
Sulphur	n/a		n/a	
Vanadium	n/a		n/a	
Zinc	15 mg		33 times RDA	

*   US (Recommended Daily Allowances) are based on estimates by the National Academy of Sciences/National Research Council.
**   Adapted from John Hathcock's "Quantitative Evaluation of Vitamin Safety," Pharmacy Times, May 1985.
***   Estimate only — from global health research on data available.
**** Usual therapeutic dose.
RDAs and Margin of Allowances courtesy of the "Natural Life Magazine" Burnaby, B.C., Canada.

Vitamins

Vitamin	Natural Sources	Affected Components
A Fat soluble RDA 4000 IU.	Fish liver oils, beef and chicken liver, carrots, beets, green leafy vegetables (kale, turnip greens, spinach), Colorado fruits, melon, squash, yams, butter, tomatoes, margarine, cod liver oil, spirulina, watercress, cheese, and other dairy products.	Bones, eyes, hair, mucous linings and membranes, immune system, adrenal glands, nails, skin cells, and teeth.
B1 **Thiamin** Water soluble RDA - 1.4 mg.	Brewers yeast, wheat germ, rice polishings, all seeds, nuts and nut butters, soy beans, oat meal, asparagus, beets, potatoes, leafy green vegetables, plums, prunes, raisins, milk and dairy products, liver, poultry, egg yolks, and fish.	Brain, ears, eyes, hair, heart, nervous system, and muscles.
B2 **Riboflavin** Water soluble RDA - 1.7 mg.	Milk, cheese, and other dairy products, beef liver and kidney, yogurt, fish, egg yolks, whole grains, enriched cereals and breads, brewers yeast, torula yeast, wheat germ, almonds, sunflower seeds, currants, asparagus, broccoli, and cooked leafy vegetables.	Eyes, skin, nails, and hair.
B3 **Niacin** Water soluble RDA - 16 mg.	Liver, lean meat, white meat of poultry, kidney, fish, eggs, roasted peanuts, avocados, dates, figs, prunes, green vegetables, whole wheat products, brewers yeast, torula yeast, wheat germ, rice bran, rice polishings, and sunflower seeds.	Brain, gastro-intestinal tract, nervous system, sexual organs, heart, liver, and skin.

Functions	DeficiencySymptom	Therapeutic Uses
Aids visual purple production (necessary for night vision), promotes growth and vitality, resists infection, repairs and maintains body tissue, helps heal gastrointestinal ulcers, and helps prevent aging.	Allergies, appetite loss, blemishes, dry hair, fatigue, itching/burning eyes, loss of smell, night blindness, rough dry skin, sinus trouble, soft tooth enamel, and susceptibility to infections.	Acne, alcoholism, allergies, cancer, arthritis, asthma, athletes foot, boils, bronchitis, colds, cystitis, diabetes, carbuncles, eczema, heart disease, HIV, gum disorders, peptitis, migraine headaches, and stress.
Increase, appetite, blood building, carbohydrate metabolism, circulation, can aid digestion, energy, growth, learning capacity, prevents liquid retention, prevents constipation, and muscle tone.	Appetite loss, beriberi, digestive disturbances, fatigue, irritability, muscular weakness, nervousness, fever, numbness of hands and feet, mental depression, pains around heart, and short breath.	Alcoholism, anemia, congestive heart failure, fluid retention, constipation, diarrhea, diabetes, indigestion, lead poisoning, nausea, pain, rapid heart rate, and emotional stress.
Aids growth and reproduction, alleviates eye fatigue, antibody & red blood cell formation, promotes healthy skin, nails and hair, stimulates metabolism maintenance of the epithelial tissue.	Bloodshot and burning eyes, cataracts, corner of mouth cracks & sores, dizziness, poor digestion, premature wrinkles, a weak immune system, retarded growth, and red sore tongue.	Arteriosclerosis, baldness, cholesterol (high), cystitis, facial oiliness, hypoglycemia, light sensitivity, mental retardation, muscular disorders, nervous disorders, and nausea in pregnancy, and stress..
Circulation, lowers, cholesterol level, dilates blood vessels, hydrochloric acid production, aids metabolism (protein, fat carbohydrate), helps tone the nervous system, and increases sex hormone production.	Appetite loss, canker sores, cold feet and hands, depression, fatigue, halitosis, headaches, indigestion, insomnia, memory loss, muscular weakness, nausea, nervous disorders, pellagra, and skin eruptions.	Acne, baldness, canker sores, arthritis, diarrhea, halitosis, high blood pressure, leg cramps, stress, cancer, migraine headaches, schizophrenia, poor circulation, nervous system, memory loss, and tooth decay.

71

Vitamins continued

Vitamin	Natural Sources	Affected Components
B5 **Pantothenic Acid** Water soluble RDA - 10 mg.	Green vegetables, peas and beans, kale, cauliflower, peanuts, crude molasses, liver, kidney, pork, beef, saltwater fish, egg yolk, royal jelly, brewers yeast, wheat germ, sweet potatoes, wheat bran, whole grain breads and cereals, and brown rice.	Brain, digestive system, adrenal glands, immune system, and skin.
B6 **Pyridoxin** Water soluble RDA - 2 mg.	Brewers yeast, bananas, avocados, wheat germ, wheat bran, cantaloupe, milk, eggs, beef, liver, kidney, heart, herring, salmon, blackstrap molasses, soybeans, walnuts, peanuts, pecans, green leafy vegetables, green peppers and carrots.	Blood, muscles, nerves, and skin.
B9 **Folic Acid** Water soluble RDA-200 mcg	Brewers yeast, wheat germ, mushrooms, nuts, whole wheat, broccoli, asparagus, lima beans, lettuce, spinach, beet greens, beef and pork liver and kidney, sweet potatoes, salmon, and deep green leafy vegetables.	Blood, cells, lymph glands, hair, liver and skin.
B12 **Cobalami** Water soluble RDA - 6 mcg.	Comfrey leaves, kelp, bananas, peanuts, concord grapes, sunflower seeds, brewers yeast, wheat germ, bee pollen, lamb and beef kidney, liver, beef, pork, egg yolk, milk, cheese, clams, oysters, crab, sardines, and salmon.	Red blood cells, nervous system, and brain.

Functions	DeficiencySymptom	Therapeutic Uses
Aids in wound healing, antibody formation, carbohydrate and fat production, improves immune responses, protein conversion (energy), growth stimulation, and vitamin utilization.	Blood and skin disorders, constipation, diarrhea, duodenal ulcers, eczema, hypoglycemia, aids intestinal disorders, kidney trouble, loss of hair, cramps, premature aging, respiratory infections, and nerve problems.	Allergies, asthma, arthritis, baldness, cystitis, aids digestive disorders, duodenal ulcers, hypoglycemia, tooth decay, heart diseases, lupus, stress, anxiety, depression, and to lower blood cholesterol levels.
Alleviates nausea, antibody formation, digestion (hydrochloric acid production), fat and protein utilization (weight control), and maintains sodium and potassium balance (nerves), and improves immune response.	Acne, anemia, arthritis, convulsions in babies, depression, dizziness, nervous disorders, hair loss, irritability, learning disabilities, muscle spasms, urination problems, and muscle weakness.	Alcoholism, allergies, anemia, arthritis, bronchial asthma, bursitis, epilepsy, fatigue, glossitis, hypoglycemia, insomnia, premenstrual edema, neuritis, overweight, shingles, stress, and seborrhea.
Analgesic for pain, appetite, body growth & reproduction, division of body cells, hydrochloric acid production, improves lactation, protein metabolism, and red blood cell formation.	Folic acid anemia, canker sores, digestive disturbances, graying hair, growth problems, impaired circulation, fatigue, emotional and /or physical stress, anxiety, and mental depression.	Anemia, arteriosclerosis, baldness, cholesterol (high), constipation, heart disease, spina bifida, loss of libido, aids cervical dysplasia, overweight, and macro cystic anemia.
Appetite, proper blood cell formation, cell longevity, helps increase energy and memory, aids nervous system, metabolism (fat, protein), promotes growth, and cancer prevention.	Acute or chronic intestinal malabsorption, chronic fatigue and general weakness, intense nervousness, pernicious anemia, poor appetite, and walking and speaking difficulties.	B12 anemia, baldness, cancer, brain damage, dermatitis, eczema, leg cramps, anxiety and depression, malabsorption, physical and emotional stress, and pernicious anemia.

Vitamins continued

Vitamin	Natural Sources	Affected Components
B13 Orotic Acid Calcium orotate RDA - N/A	Root vegetables, whey, the liquid portion of soured or curdled milk.	Cells, and liver.
B15 Calcium Pangamate Water soluble RDA - 50 mg.	Whole grains, whole brown rice, pumpkin seeds, sesame seeds, nuts, and brewers yeast.	Kidneys, glands, heart, and nerves.
B17 Laetrile Nitrilosides RDA - .25 g.	Whole seeds — apricot, peach and plum pits, mung beans, lima beans, garbanzos, blackberries, blueberries, cranberries, raspberry and flaxseed.	Not known.
Biotin **B Complex** Water soluble RDA-250 mcg	Brewers yeast, fruits, nuts, soybeans, navy beans, whole grains, cauliflower, broccoli, legumes, un-polished rice, beef and beef liver and kidney, saltwater fish, egg yolk, milk, and cheese..	Hair, skin, and muscles.
Choline **B Complex** Water soluble RDA- 900 mg.	Granular or liquid lecithin, brewers yeast, wheat germ, whole grain cereals, milk, egg yolk, beef liver, beef, pork, poultry, and green leafy vegetables.	Brain, hair, gallbladder, kidneys, liver, thymus gland, and controls cholesterol buildup.
Inositol **B Complex** Water soluble RDA- 250 mg.	Liver, brewers yeast, beef brains and heart, cabbage, citrus fruits, strawberries, raspberries, cantaloupe, raisins, wheat germ, whole grains, peanuts, lecithin, milk, and unrefined molasses.	Brain, heart, kidneys, liver muscles, hair and skin.

Functions	DeficiencySymptom	Therapeutic Uses
Essential for the biosynthesis of nucleic acid, and regenerative processes in cells.	Not known.	Multiple sclerosis.
Aids recovery from fatigue, cell oxidation and respiration, metabolism (protein, fat, sugar), glandular and nervous system stimulation.	Heart problems or disease, nervous and glandular disorders.	Alcoholism, asthma, arteriosclerosis, cholesterol (high), emphysema, heart disease, headaches, hypoxia, insomnia, circulation, and rheumatism.
Purported to have cancer controlling and preventive properties.	May lead to diminished resistance to malignancies.	Cancer.
Antiseptic, encourages cell growth and fatty acid production, hair growth, and assists metabolism (carbohydrate, fat, protein), and vitamin B utilization.	Dandruff, depression, dry skin, fatigue, grayish skin, heart abnormalities, color, insomnia, muscular pain, and poor appetite.	Alcoholism, arteriosclerosis, cholesterol (high), constipation, dizziness, eczema, ear noises, dermatitis, hardening of the arteries, and high blood pressure.
Controls cholesterol buildup, lecithin formation, liver and gall bladder regulation, lowers blood pressure, metabolism (fats, cholesterol), and nerve transmission.	Bleeding stomach ulcers, cirrhosis, growth problems, heart trouble, high blood pressure, impaired liver & kidney function, and intolerance to fats.	Alcoholism, anemia, arteriosclerosis, Alzheimer's disease, baldness, cirrhosis, diarrhea, fatigue, menstrual problems, mental illness, stomach ulcers, and stress.
Artery hardening retardation, calming effect, cholesterol reduction, hair growth, lecithin formation, metabolism (fat & cholesterol), preventing eczema.	Cholesterol (high), constipation, eczema, eye abnormalities, and hair loss.	Treats eczema, neuralgic disorders and facial twitches, used for tardive dyskinesia, obesity, schizophrenia baldness, high blood pressure, and poor circulation.

Vitamins continued

Vitamin	Natural Sources	Affected Components
Paba - *B* Complex Water soluble RDA- 100 mg.	Beef liver, kidney, molasses, brewers yeast, rice bran, whole grains, wheat germ, green vegetables, peas, beans, peanuts, and egg yolk.	Hair, skin, intestines, nervous system, and thyroid gland.
C Ascorbic Acid Water soluble RDA - 60 mg.	Rose hips, citrus fruits, apples, black currants, strawberries, horseradish, beet greens, spinach, cabbage, broccoli, brussels sprouts, cauliflower, persimmons, kale, guavas, tomatoes, sweet potatoes, turnip greens, parsley, kohlrabi, collards, chives, green bell lima beans, peppers, papaya, watercress, swiss chard, and squash.	Ligaments, bones, skin, gums, heart, teeth, blood, adrenal glands, and capillary walls.
D Ergosterol Water soluble RDA - 400 IU.	Egg yolks, butter, fish liver oils, sardines, herring, halibut, salmon, tuna, sea bass, swordfish, sable, sprouted seeds, mushrooms, sweet potatoes, sunflower seeds and D fortified milk.	Bones, heart, nerves, skin, teeth, and thyroid gland.
E Tocopherol Fat soluble RDA - 15 IU.	Wheat germ, whole wheat products, brussel sprouts, corn, leafy dark green vegetables, spinach, whole wheat, whole grain cereals, vegetable oils, soy beans, safflower, brown rice nuts, egg yolks, red meats, and dairy products	Blood vessels, heart, liver, lungs, skin, adrenal and pituitary glands, testes, uterus and fatty tissues.

Functions	DeficiencySymptom	Therapeutic Uses
An antioxidant, aids in reproductive disorders, blood cell formation, graying hair, (color restoration), intestinal bacteria activity protein metabolism, and reduces pain from burns.	Anemia, constipation, depression, digestive disorders, fatigue, gray hair, headaches, irritability, and loss of libido.	Anemia, baldness, graying hair, overactive thyroid, gland all parasitic diseases, rheumatic low fever, stress, infertility. External: burns, dry skin, sunburn, and wrinkles.
Accelerates healing after surgery, bone and tooth formation, collagen production, common cold prevention, digestion, heals wounds, burns, and bleeding gums, iodine conservation, red blood cell formation, shock, and resistance against infection protection against cancer-producing agents.	Anemia, hemorrhages, allergies, capillary wall ruptures, bruise easily, dental cavities, low infection resistance (flu) (colds) etc, premature aging, poor digestion, soft and bleeding gums, thyroid insufficiency, fatigue, scurvy, and slow wound healing.	Alcoholism, asthma, arteriosclerosis, high levels of stress, arthritis, cholesterol (high), colds, cystitis, hypoglycemia, heart disease, hepatitis, insect bites, connective tissue repair, pyorrhea, prickly heat, scurvy, sinusitis, cancer prevention, bleeding gums, and tooth decay.
Aids in assimilating vitamin A, calcium & phosphorus metabolism (bone, teeth, heart action, nervous system maintenance, normal blood clotting, skin respiration.	Diarrhea, insomnia, myopia, muscular weakness, nervousness, premature aging, poor metabolism, softening bones and teeth, tooth decay, and growing problems.	Acne alcoholism, allergies, high blood pressure, arthritis, cystitis, pyorrhea, acute psoriasis, osteomalacia, osteoporosis, and rickets.
A anti - coagulant, antioxidant, alleviates fatigue, dilates blood vessels, good for blood cholesterol reduction, improves circulation, fertility, male potency, lung protection muscle and nerve maintenance, dissolves blood clots, and hot flashes.	Anemia, dry, dull or falling hair, enlarged prostrate gland, gastrointestinal disease, heart disease, impotency, premature aging, high cholesterol levels, miscarriages, muscular wasting and abnormal reflexes, sterility, and tooth decay.	All allergies, cancer, aging, arteriosclerosis, baldness, blood clots, blood cholesterol high, cystitis, diabetes, for celiac disease, menopausal and menstrual disorders, migraine headaches, myopia, phlebitis, stress, sterility, thrombosis, and varicose veins..

Vitamins continued

Vitamin	Natural Sources	Affected Components
F Linolenic and Linolic Fat soluble RDA- 100 mg.	Vegetable oils — wheat germ, almonds, avocados, peanuts, sunflower seeds, walnuts, parsley, soybeans, safflower linseed oil and herring, salmon, tuna, cod, mackerel, and shrimp.	Adrenal and thyroid glands, cells, hair, nerves, skin, heart and arteries.
H Biotin RDA-250 mcg	Brewers yeast, whole wheat flour, fruits, nuts, soybeans, unpolished rice, egg yolk, milk, saltwater fish, chicken, lamb, pork, beef, veal liver, and kidney.	Hair, skin, and muscles.
K **Menadione** Fat soluble RDA- 65 mcg.	Kelp, alfalfa, beef liver, cheese, yogurt, egg yolk, safflower and soybean oil, fish liver oil, vegetable oils, turnip greens, tomatoes, whole wheat, and leafy green vegetables.	Blood, bones, and liver.
P Rutin **Bioflavonoids** Water soluble RDA - 12 mg.	Grape seed extract, apricots, Saskatoon berries blue berries, blackberries, cherries, buck wheat and the white skins and segment part of all citrus fruit.	Blood, bones, capillary walls, gums, ligaments, skin, and teeth.
T Sesame Seed Factor	Sesame seeds, sesame butter, and egg yolks.	Blood.
U Fat soluble RDA - N/A	Raw cabbage juice, fresh cabbage, and sauerkraut.	Stomach.

Functions	DeficiencySymptom	Therapeutic Uses
Burns, saturated fat reduction, blood coagulation, blood pressure normalizer, cholesterol destroyer, combats most heart diseases, influences glandular activities, promotes healthy hair and vital organ restoration	Acne, allergies, diarrhea, dry skin, dry brittle hair, eczema, falling hair, gall stones, kidney disorders, nail problems, prostrate disorders, underweight, and varicose veins.	Acne, allergies, baldness, bronchial asthma, cholesterol (high), eczema, gall bladder and kidney problems or removal, heart disease, leg ulcers, psoriasis, rheumatoid arthritis, over and underweight.
Antiseptic, cell growth, fatty acid production, also encourages, hair growth, metabolism (carbohydrate, fat, and protein), and vitamin B utilization.	Dandruff, depression, dry skin, fatigue, grayish skin, heart abnormalities, pale skin color, insomnia, muscular pain, and poor appetite.	Alcoholism, arteriosclerosis, cholesterol (high), constipation, dizziness, eczema, ear noises, dermatitis, and hardening of the arteries, and high blood pressure.
Necessary for bone formation, activates energy producing tissues, blood clotting (coagulation), and is important for normal liver function.	Blood-clotting difficulty, bleeding ulcers, diarrhea, increased tendency to hemorrhage and miscarriages, lowered vitality, and nose bleeds.	Bruising, eye hemorrhages, celiac disease, colitis, gall stones, hemorrhaging, all menstrual problems, preparing women for childbirth, and ulcers.
Aids in healing bleeding gums, blood vessel wall maintenance, bruising minimization, cold and flu prevention, also treats nervous system, and used for capillary maintenance.	Bleeding gums, cirrhosis of the liver, eczema, hemorrhaging, hardening of arteries, and respiratory infections.	Asthma, bleeding gums, colds, eczema, edema, dizziness (caused by inner ear infections), hemorrhoids, high blood pressure, hypertension, miscarriages, rheumatism, and varicose veins.
Combats anemia and hemophilia, memory aid.	Not known.	Anemia and hemophilia.
Promotes healing in peptic ulcers.	Not known.	Peptic ulcers and duodenal ulcers.

Minerals

Mineral	Natural Sources	Affected Components
Boron RDA - 3 mg.	Leafy vegetables, potatoes, parsnips, carrots, beets and beet tops, salt water fish, tomatoes, legumes, nuts, fruits, summer squash, and whole grains.	Bones and muscles.
Calcium RDA - 800 to 1200 mg.	Carob, milk, cheese, dairy produce, sardines, salmon, clams, oysters, soybeans, kelp, dark leafy vegetables, sesame seeds, oats, navy beans, almonds, millet, walnuts, peanuts, sunflower seeds, kale, eggs, tofu, beet tops, turnip greens, asparagus, broccoli, and tortillas.	Bones, teeth, nails, blood, heart, skin, and soft tissue.
Chlorine RDA- 500 mg.	Kelp. watercress, avocado, chard, cabbage, kale, celery, asparagus, cucumber, olives, tomatoes, turnip, and fish.	Blood, cells, liver, and stomach.
Chromium RDA-200 mcg.	Brewers yeast, cane sugar, meat, shell fish, chicken, clams, whole grain cereals, dried beans, cheese, potatoes, sunflower and corn oil.	Arteries, blood and heart.
Cobalt RDA - 8 mcg.	All green leafy vegetables, beef or pork kidney and liver, poultry, clams, oysters, saltwater fish, milk, and lean red meat.	Blood, bone marrow, digestive system, and nervous system.
Copper RDA - 2 mg.	Beef liver and kidney, poultry, eggs, clams, oysters, lobster, crab, almonds, peanuts, dried peas and beans, avocados and legumes, prunes, plums, cherries, citrus fruits, raisins, whole grain products, oats, and green leafy vegetables.	Blood, bones, brain, connective tissues, heart, kidney, liver, and nerves.

Functions	DeficiencySymptom	Therapeutic Uses
A hormone regulator, increases testosterone levels, maintains bone strength and promotes muscle growth, and improves brain function.	Calcium loss and bone demineralization.	Builds muscles, helps prevent osteoporosis, arthritis, strengthens the immune system, and treats bacterial and fungal infections.
Helps bone and tooth formation, blood clotting, heart rhythm, nerve tranquilization, nerve transmission, useful in muscle growth and contraction, helps reduce colon cancer incidence, and can prevent osteoporosis.	Heart palpitations, high blood pressure, muscle cramping, irritability, nervousness, arm and leg numbness, abnormal tooth decay, softening of bone, susceptibility to bone fractures, and insomnia.	For arthritis, aging symptoms (backache, bone pain, finger tremors, foot and leg cramps, insomnia, menstrual cramps, menopause problems, nervousness, overweight, rheumatism, hypertension, rickets, colitis, and cancer.
Maintains fluid and electrolyte balance, helps liver, and the production of hydrochloric acid.	Impaired digestion, loss of hair and teeth, derangement of fluid levels in the body.	Digestion, stomach acidity, loss of hair and teeth, stiffness of joints, pH and enzyme activator.
Regulates blood sugar levels and glucose metabolism (energy), also can help the synthesis of proteins.	Arteriosclerosis, heart disorders, glucose intolerance in diabetics, memory loss, and depressed growth rate.	Diabetes and hypoglycemia, fatigue, heart disease, muscle loss, high cholesterol, aids growth, and treats infections.
Aids in hemoglobin formation, helps reduce blood pres-sure, and maintains a healthy nervous system.	Development of pernicious anemia, high blood pressure, and fatigue.	Anemia, production of red blood cells, and reduces high blood pressure. .
Development of bones, brain, nerves, and the connective tissues, and hair, healing processes of body, helps the mental and emotional processes, hemoglobin and red blood cell formation.	General weakness, degeneration of the nervous system, reproductive problems and sterility, anemia, impaired respiration, skeletal defects and bone disease, and skin sores.	An energy booster. Used for anemia and edema, skeletal defects, cancer, rheumatoid arthritis, immune system, iron absorption, heart disorders, aneurysms, ulcers, and leukemia

81

Minerals continued

Mineral	Natural Sources	Affected Components
Fluorine RDA - 1 mg.	Milk, cheese, carrots, garlic, sunflower seeds, seafood, tea, and fluoridated drinking water.	Bones and teeth.
Germanium RDA - N/A	Garlic, aloe vera, comfrey, chorella, gin seng, meats, dairy products, watercress, suma, shiitake mush-rooms, garlic, onions, and whole wheat.	All cells.
Iodine RDA-150 mcg	Kelp, dulse and other seaweed, seafoods and salt water fish, liver oils, egg yolks, citrus fruits, artichokes, garlic, turnip greens, spinach watercress, lima beans, asparagus, summer squash, sesame seeds, mushrooms, pine-apples, pears, peaches, pumpkin, iodized salt. and sea salt.	Hair, nails, thyroid gland, brain, skin, and teeth.
Iron RDA 10 mg. Males 18 mg. Females	Apricots, fish, peaches, bananas, black molasses, prunes, raisins, figs, whole rye, walnuts, brewers yeast, kelp, dulse, dry beans and lentils, leafy vegetables, asparagus, potatoes, pork liver, beef heart and kidney, milk, egg yolks, red meat, oysters, raw clams, and whole wheat breads and cereals.	Blood, bones, nails, skin, and teeth.
Lithium RDA - N/A	Kelp, dulse, and seafood.	Nerves, muscles, and brain.

Functions	DeficiencySymptom	Therapeutic Uses
Strengthens bones, reduces tooth decay, prevents calcification of organs.	Tooth decay and bone loss.	Tooth decay, heart disease, calcification of organs, and osteo-porosis.
A relatively new mineral. builds immune cells, gives energy, and has rejuvenative properties.	Not known.	Anemia, Raynaud's disease, burns, angina, stroke, food allergies, rheumatoid arthritis, candidiasis, pain, AIDS, and chronic viral infections.
Energy production, metabolism (excess fat), relieves pain of fibrocystic breasts. physical and mental development., regulate the functioning of the nervous system, and determines the level of body metabolism . and helps protect against thyroid damage.	Cold hands and feet, dry hair, irritability, nervousness, mental fatigue, swelling of thyroid, and obesity.	Arteriosclerosis, hair and nail problems, goiter, fibrocystic breasts, respiratory problems, mental retardation, to help increase energy, obesity, nervousness, irritability, hearing loss, hyperthyroidism, and muscle and circulatory activity.
Supports hemoglobin production, stress and disease resistance, also supports growth and development in children, prevents and cures iron-deficiency anemia, increases white blood cell count, boosts energy, helps maintain function of the immune system, and helps protein metabolism.	Breathing difficulties, brittle nails, iron deficiency, intellectual impairment, intolerance to cold, anemia (pale skin, chronic fatigue), constipation, poor attention span, and weakened immune system.	Alcoholism, iron deficiency anemia, colitis, the immune system, to maintain energy levels, helps headaches, fatigue, listlessness, learning problems, irritability, reduced white blood cell count, heart palpitations during exertion, pale color, and used to treat menstrual problems.
Helps transport sodium metabolism to brain nerves and muscles.	Nervous and mental disorders.	Paranoid schizophrenic.

Minerals continued

Mineral	Natural Sources	Affected Components
Magnesium RDA-350 mg.	Apples, figs, lemons, peaches, kale, endive, chard, celery, alfalfa, beet tops, whole grains, brown rice, sesame seeds, sunflower seeds, almonds, yellow corn, shellfish, salmon, liver, soybeans, brewer's yeast and honey.	Arteries, bones, blood, heart, muscles, nerves, and teeth.
Manganese RDA - 3 mg.	Nuts and whole grains, spinach, beets and beet leaves, brussel sprouts, peas, kelp, wheat germ, tea, apricots, blueberries, bananas, citrus fruits, nuts, and egg yolks.	Brain, thyroid and mammary glands, muscles, and nerves.
Molybdenum RDA - .15 mg.	Brown rice, millet, buck wheat, legumes, leafy vegetables, brewers yeast, and whole grain cereals.	Blood.
Phosphorus RDA - 800 to 1200 mg.	Milk and other dairy products, hard cheeses, cereals, whole grains, seeds and nuts, egg, canned fish, poultry, meat, yeast, wheat germ, dried fruits, legumes, corn, and carbonated soft drinks.	Bones, brain, cell walls, heart, kidneys, nerves, and teeth.
Potassium RDA - 2000 to 2500 mg.	All vegetables, bananas, citrus fruits, cantaloupe, dried apricots, tomatoes, water cress, sunflower seeds, whole grains and cereals, peanut, butter, mint leaves, potatoes, milk and dairy products - except cheese, beef liver, poultry, pork, veal, tuna, salmon, halibut, mackerel, oysters, clams, and crab.	Blood, heart, kidneys, muscles, nerves, and skin.

Functions	DeficiencySymptom	Therapeutic Uses
Acid /alkaline balance, essential in blood sugar metabolism (energy), metabolism of calcium and vitamin C, and is involved in structuring of basic genetic material.	Confusion, fatigue, disorientation, easily aroused anger, nervousness, rapid pulse, premenstrual tension, tremors and muscle tension and cramps, weakness and hyperactivity in children.	Alcoholism, cholesterol problems, depression, acute heart conditi-ons, kidney or gall stones, nervousness, prostrate troubles, sensitivity to noise, stomach acidity, tooth decay, and overweight.
Enzyme activation, reproduction & growth, sex hormone production, tissue respiration, vitamin B1 metabolism, and vitamin E utilization.	Ataxia (muscle co-ordination failure), dizziness, ear noises, glucose intolerance, and loss of hearing.	Allergies, asthma, diabetes, Alzheimer's disease and epileptic seizures, nervous disorders, sexual dysfunction, fatigue., and retarded growth.
Integral part of enzymes involved in oxidation processes. and urea production.	Decreased ability to metabolize fats and carbohydrates.	Copper poisoning, impotence in men, anemia, dental caries, and cancer.
Bone/tooth formation, cell growth and repair, energy production, helps heart muscle contraction, kidney function, metabolism, nerve and muscle activity.	Appetite loss, fatigue, irregular breathing, acute nervousness, muscle cramps, bone problems and disorders, blurred vision, overweight, and / or weight loss.	Arthritis, stunted growth in children, stress, tooth and gum disorders and mental and / or nervous disorders.
Regulates heartbeat, slows rapid growth, helps relax muscle contractions, converts glucose into glycogen, reduces swelling in the extremities, nerve tranquilization, protects and controls the activity of the kidneys, body fluids, and acid balance.	Acne, alcoholism or continuous thirst, dry skin, loss of appetite, constipation, general weakness, insomnia, muscle damage, nervousness, irritability, anorexia nervosa, slow or irregular heartbeat, vomiting, sweating, and slow or weak reflexes.	Acne, alcoholism, allergies, all burns, insomnia, colic in infants, diabetes, high blood pressure, heart disease (angina pectoris, congestive heart failure, an irregular pulse, and myocardial infraction), nausea stroke, constipation, and cancer.

Minerals continued

Mineral	Natural Sources	Affected Components
Selenium RDA - .05 mg.	Wheat germ, brown rice, soybeans, Brazil nuts, brewers yeast, kelp, garlic, mushrooms, pineapples, onions, tomatoes, broccoli, saltwater fish, clams, beef liver, heart, milk, and bran.	Blood, tissues, cells, prostrate gland, kidneys, liver, spleen, pancreas, and testicles.
Silicon RDA - N/A	Flaxseed, steel cut oats, whole grains, almonds, peanuts, sunflower seeds, celery, apples, straw-berries, grapes, kelp, beets, onions, parsnips, and hard drinking water.	Bones, hair, nails, and teeth.
Sodium RDA-1100 mg	Sea salt, kelp, saltwater fish, shellfish, carrots, celery, asparagus, romaine lettuce, beets, chicken, beef, pork, eggs, milk, dried beef, brains, kidney, and watermelon.	Blood, lymph system, stomach, muscles, and nerves.
Sulfur RDA - N/A	Radish, turnip, onions, celery, horseradish, kale, soybeans, cucumber, water cress, milk, eggs, fish, poultry, and beef.	Hair, skin, nails, and nerves.
Vanadium RDA - N/A	Fish, parsley, radishes, straw-berries, lettuce, and cucumber peels.	Heart and blood vessels.
Zinc RDA - 15 mg.	Sprouted seeds, wheat bran and germ, pumpkin seeds, sunflower seeds, brewers yeast, onions, nuts, green leafy vegetables, peas, beets and beet tops, carrots, lean beef, beef or pork liver, lamb chops, pork loin, poultry, milk and cheese, clams, lobster, crab, sardines and herring.	Blood, bone, brain, heart, liver, muscle, and prostrate gland.

Functions	DeficiencySymptom	Therapeutic Uses
Antioxidant and anti-cancer mineral, slows aging process and hardening of tissues through oxidation, helps stimulate immune system and liver functions.	Premature stamina loss, poor tissue repair, dry flaky scalp, hair loss, skin problems, chest pains, free radical damage, and liver cancer.	A degenerated liver function, arthritis, mercury poisoning, and heart male potency, hot flushes during menopause, liver cancer, and all circulatory diseases.
Building of strong bones, helps healing process and builds immune system, assists in the utilization of calcium, and is involved in maintain-ing the normal growth of hair, nails and teeth.	Aging symptoms of skin (wrinkles), thin-ning or loss of hair, poor bone development, soft or brittle nails, insomnia, con-nective tissue disorder, muscle cramps, and irritability.	Hair loss, irritations in mucous membranes, skin disorders, the immune system, and insomnia.
Helps nerves and muscles function prop-erly and normalizes glandular secretions, and regulates electro-lites, pH, body fluid volume and blood.	Excessive sweating, chronic diarrhea, nausea, respiratory failure, heat exhaustion, and impaired carbohydrate digestion.	Sun stroke, heat prostration, muscular weakness, and mental apathy.
Collagen synthesis and body tissue formation and enhances nerve structure formation.	Not known.	Arthritis. mental and nervous disorders, menopausal problems, External: skin disorders.
Inhibits cholesterol formation in the blood vessels.	High blood pressure, and hardening of the arteries.	Prevents heart attacks and high blood pressure.
Speeds the burn and / or wound healing process, encourages carbohydrate digest-ion, prostrate gland function, reproductive organ growth and development, sex organ growth and maturity, and helps vitamin B1, and protein metabolism.	A delayed sexual maturity, fatigue, loss of taste, poor appetite, prolonged wound healing, retarded growth, poor sex drive, sterility, prostate problems, joint pains, acne, and recurrent infections.	Alcoholism, arterio-sclerosis, poor sense of taste and smell, baldness, cirrhosis, diabetes, internal and external wound and injury healing, high cholesterol, skin rash, retarded growth and development, and infertility.

Other Supplements

Other Sups.	Natural Sources	Affected Components
Acidophilus (Flora)	Natural "live" yogurt, also known as "bio yogurt".	Intestines, kidney, bowel, skin, and sexual organs.
Antler Horn (Velvet)	Powdered Deer or Elk horns,	The immune system, blood, and intestines, sexual organs.
Bee Pollen (Honey)	Unpasteurized honey contains small amounts of bee pollen. Bee pollen contains protein, amino acids, sugar, and small amounts of vitamins, minerals, and enzymes.	The entire body.
Bio-flavonoids (Flavones)	Apricots, cherries, citrus fruit peel, broccoli, green peppers, and the central white core of lemons, limes, and oranges.	Capillaries, veins, and arteries
Brewer's Yeast	From hops - a by-product of beer.	Lymph nodes, skin, and neural system.
Cellulose	Apples , bran, brussel sprouts, carrots, cabbage, cucumber skins, green beans, peas, and peppers.	Colon and large bowel.

Functions	DeficiencySymptom	Therapeutic Uses
Keeps the intestines clean and maintains intestinal health. Aids absorption of nutrients in food and reduces blood cholesterol levels.	Irritability and depression, fatigue, and acute intestinal problems.	Constipation and flatulence, acne and other skin troubles, high cholesterol. yeast infections, candida, and bad breath.
Reduces side effects of chemo-therapy, contains, anabolic and growth properties, treats a variety of degenerative diseases, helps increase muscle strength and endur-ence, stimulates the immune system,	Sexual disorders, skin complaints, and weak immune system.	Skin ulcers, psoriasis, lumbago, impotence in men, gastrointestinal disorders, premature ejaculation, diabetes, cold hands and feet, weak bones, memory loss, infertility, and menstrual problems.
Boosts the immune system and regulates the bowels, helps to increase athletic stamina and recovery time. and retards the aging process.	Fatigue and lack of energy.	Excellent for skin problems, prostrate problems, constipat-ion, allergies, helps to suppress appetite and encourages hair growth, and cravings.
An antioxidant, helps protect the circulatory system, helps fight viral infections, and lowers cholesterol.	Extremely susceptible to bruising.	Cerebral and other hemorrhaging, edema, inner ear infection, aging, and abnormally heavy menstruation.
Rich in vitamins, amino acids, and nucleic acids, a good energy builder, and it boosts the activity of the immune system.	Lack of energy, weakened immune system, and fatigue.	Wrinkling and other skin problems, the healing of burns, bruises, and wounds, mental efficiency, and helps strengthen the immune system.
Absorbs water and moves waste through the colon more rapidly.	Constipation.	Diverticulosis, cancer of the colon, spastic colon, hemorrhoids, and varicose veins.

Other Supplements

Other Sups.	Natural Sources	Affected Components
Charcoal	Burned cellulose, peat, wood, and bituminous coal.	Blood and intestines.
Chlorophyll (Chlorella) (Kyo-green)	Barley leaves or algae.	Blood, cells, immune system, and intestines.
Co-enzyme Q 10	Beef and beef hearts, pork, poultry, sardines, peanuts, beet leaves, and spinach.	All body cells.
Cyto Chrome C	Amino acids and iron.	Cells, and muscles.
Desiccated Liver	Concentrated dried liver from organically grown beef.	Blood and liver.
DHEA (Hormone)	Mexican wild yam.	Blood, heart, veins, immune system, and nervous system.
Dietary Fiber (Bulk)	Products made from apples, nuts and young peas, green beans, wax beans, broccoli, brussels sprouts, carrots, peppers, and whole grain cereal and bread.	Blood and intestines.

Functions	DeficiencySymptom	Therapeutic Uses
Acts as an antacid, absorbs gas, a cleansing effect on the bowel and intestines, and reduces blood cholesterol.	Sluggish circulation, bowel and intestinal problems.	Atherosclerosis, gas, bloating, flatulence, kidney problems, and (IBS) - irritable bowel syndrome.
High in RNA and DNA. An excellent blood cleanser and tonic, also used to chelate toxins in the digestive system, and to improve athletic performance.	Stress, indigestion, ulcerative lesions, bad breath, and a weak immune system.	Ultraviolet radiation, to accelerate wound healing, strengthen the immune system, detoxify the body, obesity, arthritis, pain, pancreatitis, and candida albicans.
It stimulates the electron flow in the cells during the process of energy production.	Muscle weakness and slowed mental and nerve reactions.	Immune system, heart failure or arrhythmia, nervous system, cell damage, lack of energy, and aging.
Increases energy and muscle performance, and carries oxygen to the mitochondria.	Lack of energy.	Treats lactic acid buildup.
Aids in building healthy red blood cells and strengthens liver functions.	Anemia.	Stress in the body, liver problems, and anemia.
Therapeutic benefits in the prevention and treatment of cancer and blood and nerve conditions.	Not available.	To strengthen the immune system, aging, weight gain, acute and chronic stress, lupus, and treating cancer.
Helps regulate sugar in the blood, reduces the production of cholesterol, and helps control weight.	Bowel irregularity and constipation.	Arteriosclerosis, heart diseases, cancer of the colon, diverticulosis, diabetes, and weight control.

Other Supplements

Other Sups.	Natural Sources	Affected Components
Digestive Enzymes	Avocados, bananas, and mangoes.	Blood, organs, tissues, and cells.
Evening Primrose Oil	Seeds from Evening Primrose.	Liver, skin cells, and lymph glands.
Glandulars	Beef and pork.	Blood, lungs, and muscle.
Lecithin	Soybeans, egg yolks, meat, fish, liver, cabbage, and cauliflower.	Heart, blood, liver, and nerves.
Propolis	A mixture of sticky material containing bal-sam oil, pollen, resin, and wax collected by bees to fill the cracks in their hives.	Blood and immune system.

Functions	Deficiency Symptom	Therapeutic Uses
Aid in the breakdown of proteins, fats, and carbohydrates. Necessary for proper digestion and absorption of nutrients.	Fatigue and body stress.	Pancreatic problems, gastric carcinoma, congenital achlorhy-dria, bowel regularity, stress, tension, blood cleanser, allergies, and pernicious anemia.
An anti-inflammatory, retards the aging process, converts fat into energy, lowers arterial pressure, and helps reduce the inflammation of rheumatoid arthritis.	Bloating, hormonal imbalances, water retention, depression, irritability, sjogren's syndrome, and chronic fatigue syndrome.	PMS and symptoms of menopause, eczema, psoriasis, MS in children, cirrhosis of the liver, obesity, hyperactivity, and treats abnormal cell proliferation.
Primarily used to stimulate sexual hormones, respond to stress, increase energy levels, and rejuvenate aging glands.	Premature aging, impotence, and muscle weakness.	Asthma, control the spread of cancers, hypoglycemia, hypoadrenalism, improve libido, and sexual performance.
An anti-viral, tones the nervous system, repairs the membrane-s of the liver cells, reduces high blood pressure, and enhances memory function.	Memory loss, depression, liver problems, jaundice, gallstones, and viral infections.	Viral hepatitis, manic depression, dementia, cardiovascular disease, high blood pressure, gallstones, memory loss, and Alzheimer's disease.
An antibacterial, antiviral, fungicidal and a local anesthetic. Also used to stimulate and strengthen the im-mune system, female related disorders, and to boost energy.	Susceptibility to colds inflammations, ulcers, and fatigue.	To help bruises, abrasions, wounds to heal, to help reduce the duration of colds, enhance immunity, acne, tonsillitis, ulcers, and reduce blood cholesterol levels.

Other Supplements

Other Sups.	Natural Sources	Affected Components
Royal Jelly	Secreted by salivary glands of the worker bees to develop and nurture the queen bee.	Skin, immune system, neural system, and male and female sexual organs.
Shark Cartilage	Ground cartilage extracted from sharks.	Lymph nodes, skin, muscle, bone, and sexual organs.
Seaweed (Kelp)	Seaweed's are a natural form of iodine.	Glands and intestines.
Spirulina (Algae)	Spirulina plankton or blue green algae.	The entire body.

Functions	DeficiencySymptom	Therapeutic Uses
Has a yeast inhibiting function, helps control the blood cholesterol levels, treats skin problems, also elevates testosterone levels, enhances the immune system, and improves fertility	An energy reduction, libido problems, impotence, and weakened immune system.	Arthritis, libido, acne, eczema, psoriasis, the immune system, leukemia, thrush, athlete's foot, low testosterone levels, subfertility, high cholesterol levels, and side effects of chemotherapy.
Strengthens bones and muscles, is used to enhance sexuality, boosts the immune system, an anti-inflammatory, and shrinks tumors.	A weakened immune system.	To shrink cancerous tumors, osteoarthritis, inflammation, erection problems, scleroderma, sexual problems, HIV preventative, and to treat AIDS.
The richest natural source of iodine. Has anti viral activity, reduces the effects of carcinogen, as well as radioactive materials, and a natural antacid.	Goiter or thyroid problems.	Good for goiter, exudative wounds, cancer, thyroid pro-blems, hypoglycemia, intestinal disorders - (belching, indigestion, and flatulence).
A natural antacid. Helps to counter the side effects of radiotherapy and chemotherapy treatment. It also has general rejuvenating tonic properties.	Lack of energy, diabetes, and fatigue.	Used for appetite control, skin disorders, intestinal problems, reduces the effects of carcinogen, enhance immune response, aid weight loss, and used for cancer prevention.

AROMATHERAPY & ESSENTIAL OILS

Aromatherapy is about 5000 years old. There are records of the use of herbs and oils to treat illnesses in the Egyptian papyrus. The Egyptian priests where the first to experiment with aromatics and the papyri records list myrrh as an anti-inflammatory influence. This herbal oil is still listed in texts on pharmacognosy as an anti-inflammatory.

Today the modern Aromatherapists use the volatile or essential oils extracted from herbs to treat specific ailments and restore a natural balance on both mental and physical levels.

In aromatherapy the principal methods used to encourage essential oils to enter the body are baths, compress, gargle or mouthwash, inhalation, and massage. Body massage and the internal use of concentrated essential oils treat physical problems and the use of body massage and inhalations with essential oils treat mental problems.

Essential oils can be used alone or blended with other essential oils to change the medicinal properties or actions, or create a "synergistic" blend, so the oils can work in harmony and to create a blend for therapeutic purposes.

Essential oils are highly volatile so evaporate readily when exposed to air. When inhaled they enter the body through the olfactory system and when applied to the skin they permeate through to the cell tissues and capillaries.

Points to remember:

* Always dilute essential oils before applying to the skin.
* Keep essential oils away from children.
* Do not take essential oils internally on your own initiative.
* Do not apply essential oils around the eyes.

Consult Aromatherapist, Herbalist, or Practitioner if you:

* Have high blood pressure;
* Are pregnant;
* Have a chronic medical condition;
* Are taking homeopathic remedies;
* Intend to treat infants;
* Are an alcoholic;
* Have epilepsy;
* Are on medication.

Safe essential oils - for use during pregnancy:

* Chamomile, Grapefruit, Jasmine, Lavender,
* Neroli, Rose, and Ylang Ylang.

FLOWER REMEDIES

Flower remedies are sometimes confused with essential oils because they are both derived from plants. The flower remedies are prepared in different ways from essential oils and have different ways of using the energy of plants in the treatment of illness.

Flower Remedies are not addictive, simple and safe, suitable for people of all ages, including young babies and pregnant women. If the child is breast feeding, give the remedy to the mother.

Each Flower Remedy is associated with a certain emotional state, or a personality trait. Sometimes a single flower remedy is all that is required to treat your overall temperament but if no single remedy addresses all of your concerns two or more are combined. Although there is no danger in combining more than three remedies, the effectiveness is diminished if the blend is to complicated.

BACH FLOWER REMEDIES

Dr. Edward Bach (1886 - 1936) a noted British bacteriologist, physician, homeopath, and researcher is credited with classifying thirty eight negative states of mind common to all persons and discovering thirty eight flower remedies.

The remedies he devised are used to treat physical illness by easing specific types of mental and emotional distress. The flower remedies are gentle and easy to use, unlike chemical mood altering drugs. His successors continue to make his remedies today. They are distributed under the name Bach Flower Remedies.

RESCUE FLOWER REMEDY

Of all the Bach Flower Remedies the favorite of most people is Bach's Rescue Remedy. It was researched and developed in the early 1930s. The Rescue Remedy can be bought in a cream or a liquid. It is composed of equal amounts of the five essences listed below.

Ingredients for the rescue formula:

* **CHERRY PLUM** - For irrational thoughts and desperation.

* **CLEMATIS** - For short attention span and indifference.

* **IMPATIENS** - For hyperactive behavior, and impatience.

* **ROCK ROSE** - For terror, panic, or fear.

* **STAR OF BETHLEHEM** - For emotional or physical shock.

SINGULAR FLOWER REMEDIES

AGRIMONY For those that hide their feelings of anguish behind a cheerful facade.

ASPEN For unsettling fear of the unknown - a feeling that something bad may happen.

BEECH For the perfectionist who is judgmental, hypercritical, intolerant, and has very little patience with others. Those who always look for what they can find wrong.

BLACK EYED SUSAN For workaholics who are always in a rush and expend their energy at an extremely fast rate, causing general tension, irritability, and stress.

BLUEBELL For those that are emotionally closed and have lost all warm feelings for their loved ones and people in general. This remedy brings a will to share and love.

BUSH FUCHSIA For people with learning disabilities such as Dyslexia.

CENTAURY For those who are over-anxious to serve and find it impossible to say no.

CERATO For people that lack confidence in their ability to make their own decisions.

CHERRY PLUM For those that have irrational thoughts. They are compulsive, and have difficulty controlling their actions or impulses to do things they know are wrong.

CHESTNUT BUD For those that don't learn from their own past experiences and find it hard to learn from life – usually repeat the same mistakes over and over again.

CHICORY For those overly concerned and possessive of persons close to them.

CLEMATIS For those that daydream, are absent minded, and can not concentrate.

CRAB APPLE For those that feel that they have become contaminated and need to be cleansed. They are often preoccupied with problems and unable to tolerate disorder.

ELM For those people overwhelmed with feelings of incompetence or inadequacy.

GENTAIN For those that discourage easily, having selfdoubt and at times depression.

GORSE For those with feelings of deep despair following a traumatic situation.

GRAY SPIDER FLOWER For those with intense and extreme feelings of terror.

HEATHER For those that avoid being alone, are self absorbed, and tend to talk exclusively about their own problems and concerns. They are generally self-centered.

HOLLY For those people that suffer bouts of anger, jealousy, envy, and fits of temper.

HONEYSUCKLE For those that are obsessed with the happy events of the past rather than living in the present. A good remedy for people suffering from homesickness.

HORNBEAM For those that suffer from extreme fatigue, exhaustion, and tiredness.

IMPATIENS For those with feelings of impatience, irritability, and tension.

KANGAROO PAW For those that are self-conscious and have poor social skills.

LARCH For people that feel inferior, lack self-confidence, and have low self-esteem.

MIMULUS For fear of specific and known things such as the dark, other people, being alone, and heights etc. The opposite to Aspen persons who fear unknown things.

MULLA MULLA For people suffering from burns, radiation, or heat exhaustion.

MUSTARD For those with sadness, onset of gloom, and depression without cause.

OAK For those with a relentless drive to achieve. They tirelessly struggle on despite delays, great odds, and oppositions. They never giving up when ill or exhausted.

OLIVE For people that are sapped of strength and vitality at all levels. They have no reserve energy to complete their tasks and are left physically and mentally drained.

PINE For those that blame themselves for other people's mistakes and feel guilt for their shortcomings. They fail to live up to the expectations that they set for themselves

RED CHESTNUT For those with excessive concern over the well being of family and friends. Their fear that something may happen to others causes considerable distress.

ROCK ROSE For those that have extreme states of terror, panic, hysteria, and alarm.

ROCK WATER For those that demand perfection in all others and themselves.

SCLERANTHUS For people that suffer from indecision and dramatic mood swings.

STAR OF BETHLEHEM For those with acute distress brought about by the emotional shock associated with the trauma of accidents, personal loss, or bad news.

STURT DESERT ROSE For those people with emotions of guilt, regret, and shame.

SWEET CHESTNUT For those suffering severe mental anguish and deep despair.

VERVAIN For those individuals who have a strong sense of justice with fixed ideals and principals. They are always teaching and philosophizing.

VINE For people that are utterly ruthless in the pursuit of their desires and will do and say anything to convert others to their way of thinking. Must have their own way.

WALNUT For those that are easily influenced and are in an unwanted situation.

WARATAH For people in deep despair and crises, (physical and emotional).

WATER VIOLET For those that have a tendency to be alone. They are self-reliant, aloof, prideful, and at times condescending. Have no desire to associate with others.

WEDDING BUSH For those with a pattern of starting but not finishing.

WHITE CHESTNUT For obsessive thinkers that are persistently troubled by unwanted thoughts. They have a tendency to dwell on events or ideas without letup.

WILD OAT For people that are dissatisfied with their position in life. They feel that life has passed them by and are indecisive and fearful over future plans.

WILD ROSE For those that who drift through life and accept any eventuality.

WILLOW For people with feelings of jealousy, dissatisfaction, and resentfulness.

WISTERIA For those that have problems experiencing intimacy and mutual trust.

A WORD ABOUT HERBS

SINGLE HERBS
A herb with medical properties used by Herbalists for the prevention and correction of disease. All herbs in this book are presented for the express purpose of making it easy for the layman to use.

HERBAL COMBINATIONS
Herbal combinations consist of two or more herbs selected and compounded to cover symptoms of specific diseases. A single herb often does not have all of the therapeutic qualities that are required.

HERBAL SYRUPS AND TINCTURES
When immediate results are needed, the liquid extracts are suitable because of their rapid absorption. They can be added to small amounts of juice, water, and herb teas to make them more palatable.

HERBAL DOSAGES
You should only use the dosages recommended by the manufacturer as the strengths can vary. The quantities and frequencies written on the labels are for adults weighing approximately 150 lbs. When using herbal remedies for children or the elderly, the use should be decreased. Herbal capsules may be prepared as a tea. To make sure that the herbs are properly assimilated, they should be taken with a full glass of water.

SINGLE HERBS

ALFALFA
Medicinal Parts: Flowers, Leaves, Petals, and Sprouts.
Actions and Uses: Very high in vitamin and minerals thus nourishes the entire system. Excellent for pregnant women and nursing mothers. Good for the pituitary gland. It alkalizes the body rapidly and helps detoxify the liver. Helps rebuild decayed teeth and relieve arthritic and rheumatic pain. Also aids in the assimilation of protein, fats and carbohydrates. Contains an anti fungus agent.
Bodily Influence: Nutrient, Tonic.

ALFA-MAX
Medicinal Part: Leaves.
Actions and Uses: A concentrated alfalfa extract made from the leaves of alfalfa, Alfalfa surpasses all other natural, unprocessed foods in vitamin and mineral content. Approximately one ton of green alfalfa makes 80 lbs. of Alfa-Max.
Bodily Influence: Nutrient, Tonic.

ALOE VERA
Medicinal Part: Leaves.
Actions and Uses: Aloe Vera is a potent medicine and healer. An excellent colon cleanser. Healing and soothing to the stomach as well as liver, kidneys, spleen and bladder. Also an excellent remedy for piles and hemorrhoids. Works with your immune system to keep you healthy, strong and vibrant.

Bodily Influence: Anthelmintic, Emmena- gogue, Purgative, and Tonic.

ANGELICA

Medicinal Parts: Herb, Root and Seed.
Actions and Uses: Resists poisons, aids in expulsion of gas from the stomach and intestines, also good for colic, grip and heartburn. Promotes secretion of fluid from respiratory track. Tea taken hot will quickly break up a cold.
Bodily Influence: Aromatic, Carminative, Diaphoretic, Diuretic, Emmenagogue, Expectorant, and Stimulant.

APRICOT

Medicinal Part: Kernel.
Actions and Uses: In China this herb is only used as a nutritive tonic for the lungs. In the west the apricot kernel is highly regarded as an anti-cancer source of laetrile.
Bodily Influence: Demulcent, Expectorant, and Nutritive.

ASHWAGANDHA

Medicinal Part: Leaves and Bark.
Actions and Uses: Contains a compound called *Withaferin*. This compound boosts the bodies immunity and resistance to disease, it fights tumors, viruses, bacterial, and fungal infections. This herb also improves sexual function and is used for age related learning and memory problems.
Bodily Influence: Analgestic, Anodyne, Antirheumatic, Aphrodisiac, and Nervine.

ASTRAGLUS

Medicinal Part: Root.
Actions and Uses: Strengthens the immune systems and promotes healing. It strengthens resistance to disease and improves digestion.
Bodily Influence: Anhydrotic, Diuretic, and Tonic.

BARBERRY

Medicinal Parts: Bark, Berries and Root.
Actions and Uses: and blood tonic.
External use — antiseptic root tea. Also used for kidney ailments.
Bodily Influence: Antiseptic, Laxative, Stimulant, and Tonic.

BARLEY GRASS

Medicinal Part: Leaves.
Actions and Uses: Excellent source of chlorophyll, used to treat rheumatic and arthritic symptoms. Barley water gives relief in fevers, diarrhea and stomach irritations.
Bodily Influence: Demulcent, and Nutritive.

BAYBERRY

Medicinal Part: The root bark.
Actions and Uses: Astringent and stimulant effective in cleaning congestion from the nose and sinuses. Good for all mucus membrane conditions. Made into a tea it is excellent as a gargle for sore throats. Valuable for all kinds of hemorrhages.
Bodily Influence: Astringent, Stimulant, and Tonic.

BEE POLLEN

Medicinal Part: Fresh pollen from bees.
Actions and Uses: A miracle food from nature rich in vitamins, minerals and amino acids. Reduces the craving for protein. Used for aging, prostrate gland, fatigue, allergies and as a sexual rejuvenate. Also contains natural antibodies so is effective against infections.

Bodily Influence: Antimicrobial and Antiseptic.

Warning: Some people may be allergic to bee pollen. Use small amounts at first and discontinue if discomfort or any other symptoms occur.

BEECH DROP

Medicinal Part: Whole Plant.

Actions and Uses: This herb is used by homeopaths to treat cancer, Also good for diarrhea, asthma, and is valuable in the treatment of obstinate ulcers of the mouth and stomach.

Bodily Influence: An eminent astringent.

BEET POWDER

Medicinal Part: Root.

Actions and Uses: One of the best-known plant sources of assumilable iron. Good for toning and rebuilding liver also gall bladder infections. Also contains Vitamin A, B, C, sodium, potassium, calcium and chlorine.

Bodily Influence: Adaptogen, Hepetic, and Nutritive.

BILBERRY

Medicinal Part: Leaves and Berries.

Actions and Uses: Bilberry has a well established reputation as being similar to insulin for sugar diabetes. Useful for diarrhea, dropsy, gravel, liver and stomach conditions.

Bodily Influence: Astringent, Diuretic, and Refrigerant.

BLACK COHOSH

Medicinal Part: Root.

Actions and Uses: A natural precursor to estrogen; helps relieve symptoms such as premenstrual and menstrual cramps. Lowers cholesterol and high blood pressure (equalizes circulation), helpful for poisonous bites,

reduces mucus levels, and relieves sinusitis and asthma.

Bodily Influence: Alterative, Anti-spasmodic, Cardiac Stimulant, Diuretic, Diaphoretic, Emmenagogue, Expectorant, and Sedative (arterial and nervous)

Warning: Do not take if you are pregnant or have any type of chronic disease.

BLACK WALNUT

Medicinal Parts: Bark, Husks, Leaves, Rind, and Green Nut.

Actions and Uses: Expels internal parasites and tape worms. Should be applied topically to ring worm twice a day until it disappears. Aids in treatment of tuberculosis, diarrhea, and promotes healing of sores in mouth and throat. Rich in manganese which is important for nerves, brain and cartilage, and helps relieve many kinds of skin problems.

Bodily Influence: Tonic, and Vermifuge.

BLADDERWRACK

Medicinal Parts: Leaves and Root.

Actions and Uses: Eliminates parasites, improves goiter and kidney functions, increases thyroid activity, and absorbs water in the intestines to produce bulk.

Bodily Influence: Adaptogen, and Vermifuge.

BLESSED THISTLE

Medicinal Parts: Flower, Leaves, Root, and Seed.

Actions and Uses: Stimulates appetite, promotes menstrual discharge, helps regulate hormones, increase milk production while nursing, also a stimulant to brain, circulation, heart and nerves.

Bodily Influence: Adaptogen, Galact-agogue, and Stimulant.

102

Warning: Handle carefully to avoid toxic skin effects.

BLUE COHOSH

Medicinal Part: Root.
Actions and Uses: Relieves or prevents spasms, cramps, colic, diabetes, leukorrhea, nervous disorders, rheumatism. Elevates blood pressure, cleanses blood, promotes perspiration also increases volume of urine excreted.
Bodily Influence: Antispasmodic, Depurative, Diuretic, Dysmenorrhea, Emmenagogue, Oxytocic, Parturient, Sudorific and Spasmodic.

BLUE VERVAIN

Medicinal Parts: Leaves, Root, and Stems.
Actions and Uses: Expels worms, increases and restores proper blood circulation, relieves bladder, helps to expel phlegm from the throat and lungs. Good for asthma, epilepsy, colds, female disorders, fever, flu, headaches, and pneumonia.
Bodily Influence: Antiperiodic, Anti-pasmodic, Diaphoretic, Emetic, Expectorant, Nervine, Sudorific, and Tonic.

BONESET

Medicinal Parts: Leaves and Tops.
Actions and Uses: Mild laxative, reduces fevers, promotes perspiration. Also used in the treatment of acute and chronic rheumatism.
Bodily Influence: Antispasmodic, Aperient, Diaphoretic, Emetic, Stimulant, and Tonic.

BUCHU

Medicinal Part: Leaves.
Actions and Uses: Used for chronic inflammation of the bladder, digestive disorders, irritation of the urethra, urine retention, nephritis, cystitis and catarrh of the bladder.
Bodily Influence: Antiseptic, diuretic, and stimulant,

BURDOCK

Medicinal Parts: Leaves, Seed, Stems, Root, (the whole herb).
Actions and Uses: Cleanses and eliminates impurities from the blood, thus alleviating boils, abscesses, eczema and other skin disorders. An excellent diuretic. Soothing to the kidneys. Excellent for gout and will reduce arthritic swelling, deposits within the joints.
Bodily Influence: Alterative, Diaphoretic, and Diuretic.
Warning: Burdock interferes with iron absorption.

BUTCHER'S BROOM

Medicinal Parts: Seeds, and Tops.
Actions and Uses: Builds up structure of the veins. Therefore used for hemorrhoids and other types of varicose veins. Improves poor circulation, also relieves inflammation in the kidney and bladder.
Bodily Influence: Demulcent, Mucilaginous, Rubifacient, and Styptic.

CANCER ROOT

Medicinal Part: Whole Plant.
Actions and Uses: This herb is used by homeopaths to treat cancer, Also good for diarrhea, asthma, and is valuable in the treatment of obstinate ulcers of the mouth and stomach.
Bodily Influence: Adaptogen and Astringent.

CDN. SNAKE ROOT

Medicinal Part: Root.
Actions and Uses: Accelerates childbirth causing stimulation of the involuntary muscles of the

103

uterus. Relieves gas from stomach and intestines. Promotes perspiration and increases volume of urine excreted.
Bodily Influence: Carminative, Parturient, and Stomachic.

CAPSICUM (CAYENNE)

Medicinal Part: The fruit.
Actions and Uses: A catalyst for all herbs. Capsicum taken with Burdock, Ginger, Golden Seal, Slippery elm, etc., will soon diffuse itself throughout the whole system. Improves circulation, and aids digestion. Combine with Lobelia for nerves. Unlike most stimulants of allopathy, it is not narcotic. Good for the heart, lungs kidneys, pancreas, spleen, and stomach.
Bodily Influence: Carminative, Condiment, Diaphoretic, Rubefacient, Stimulant, and Tonic.

CASCARA SAGRADA

Medicinal Part: Dried Bark.
Actions and Uses: One of the best natural laxatives in the herbal kingdom. Extremely useful in hemorrhoidal conditions and chronic constipation. It is considered suitable for delicate and elderly persons. Also a very good remedy for gallstones, increases secretion of bile.
Bodily Influence: Laxative, and Bitter tonic.

CATNIP

Medicinal Parts: The whole herb.
Actions and Uses: Excellent for small children with colic. Controls fever (catnip enemas reduce fever) Produces perspiration without increasing body temperature. Very good as a sleeping aid, relieves stress and is soothing to the nerves. Also a digestive aid for gas and diarrhea.

Bodily Influence: Antispasmodic, Aphrodisiac (cats), Carminative, Diaphoretic, Emmen-agogue, Stimulant, and Tonic.

CELERY

Medicinal Parts: Root and Seed.
Actions and Uses: Used in incontinence of dropsical, urine, and liver problems. Good for arthritis, rheumatism, neuralgia, and nervousness. Acts as an antioxidant and a sedative.
Bodily Influence: Aromatic, Carminative, Diuretic, Nerve Sedative, Stimulant, and Tonic.

CHAMOMILE

Medicinal Parts: Flowers and Herb.
Actions and Uses: A natural sedative for hysteria, nightmares, delirium and nervousness also used as a digestive aid for weak stomachs and to provide appetite.
Bodily Influence: Antispasmodic, Carmin-ative, Diaphoretic, Emmenagogue, Nervine, Sedative, and Tonic stimulant.
Warning: Do not use for long periods of time. Do not use if allergic to ragweed.

CHAPARRAL

Medicinal Parts: Leaves and Stem.
Actions and Uses: Blood purifier. One of natures best antibiotics very useful in cases of acne, arthritis, chronic backache, tumor warts and skin blotches. Protects from harmful effects of radiation and sun exposure, also used for liver problems, lymphatic troubles and digestive disorders.
Bodily Influence: Antiseptic, Diuretic, Expectorant, and Tonic.

CHASTE TREE

Medicinal Parts: Leaves and Flowers.

Actions and Uses: A hormone balancer and natural alternative to estrogen, Herbalists use Chaste Tree for the treatment of female complaints. Useful for side effects associated with menopause, fibroid tumors, and PMS.
Bodily Influence: Adaptogen, Discutient, and Nervine.

CHICKWEED

Medicinal Parts: Whole Herb.
Actions and Uses: Used extensively to help lose weight. Excellent herb for the digestive system and bowels. One of the best remedies for tumors piles and swollen testes. Excellent bronchial cleanser. Heals and soothes.
Bodily Influences: Demulcent, Emollient, Pectoral, and Refrigerant.

CHLORELLA

Medicinal Parts: Fresh spear leaves. (barley or wheat)
Actions and Uses: Highest known source of natural chlorophyll stimulates the natural immune system. Also very effective in detoxifying the liver, bloodstream and in cleansing the bowel. Chlorella helps clear heavy metals and harmful chemicals from the body.
Bodily Influences: Alterative, Depurative, Hepatic, Nutritive, and Stimulant.

CLEAVERS

Medicinal Part: Whole Herb.
Actions and Uses: Acts as a solvent of stones in the bladder. Helps with urinary secretion. Also used for treatment of scurvy, psoriasis, skin diseases and eruption generally.
Bodily Influences: Alterative, Aperient, Diuretic, Refrigerant, and Tonic.

CLUB MOSS

Medicinal Part: Whole Herb.
Actions and Uses: This herb has a naturally occurring compound called Huperzine. Huperzine is a vital brain chemical involved in memory and learning functions.
Bodily Influences: Antibiotic, Anticatarrhal, Cephalic, Febrifuge and Nutrative.

CODONOPSIS

Medicinal Part: Root.
Actions and Uses: Called "poor mans ginseng" in China. Has very similar qualities as ginseng, and can be used by both sexes in any climate.
Bodily Influences: Adaptogen and Tonic.

COLTSFOOT

Medicinal Parts: Berries and Leaves.
Actions and Uses: For congestion of the pulmonary system, especially if inclined to consumption. Also used for asthma, bronchitis, coughs, catarrh, diarrhea, fever, inflammation, and ulcers.
Bodily Influence: Demulcent, Emollient, Expectorant, Pectoral, and Tonic.
Warning: Carcinogenic properties have been discovered.

COMFREY

Medicinal Parts: Leaves and Root.
Actions and Uses: Good blood cleanser and tissue builder, help to heal broken bones, sprains and slow healing sores. Helps heal ulcers and kidney problems. Best remedy for blood in urine. Also a powerful remedy for coughs and catarrh.
Bodily Influence: Astringent, Demulcent. **Warning:** Do not use

for longer than 3 months at a time. May cause liver damage.

CORN SILK

Medicinal Part: The green pistils.

Actions and Uses: Corn Silk will assist all inflammatory conditions of the bladder, kidney, and urethra. Controls general malfunction of the body due to uric acid retention. Good for hypertension, edema, urinary tract dysfunction, and stones, bedwetting, and enlarged prostrate gland.

Bodily Influence: Alterative, Demulcent, and Diuretic.

COWSLIP

Medicinal Part: Flowers and Leaves.

Actions and Uses: Cowslip strengthens the brain and nervous systems. Highly recommended for convulsions, cramps, frenzy, false apprehension, palsy, and trembling. Also used to ease pain in the back and bladder.

Bodily Influence: Antispasmodic and Sedative.

CRANBERRY

Medicinal Part: Fruit.

Actions and Uses: Good for chronic kidney infections also used for relief of cramps and spasms of involuntary muscular contractions such as in asthma and hysteria.

Bodily Influence: Diuretic, Mucilaginous, and Nervine.

DAMIANA

Medicinal Part: Leaves.

Actions and Uses: A great sexual rejuvenator. Gives energy, helps to balance female hormones. Controls bed wetting, expels excess water from the body. Stimulates muscular contractions of the intestinal tract and increases blood circulation.

Bodily Influence: Aphrodisiac, Laxative, Stimulant, and Tonic.

Warning: Damiana interferes with iron absorption when taken internally.

DANDELION

Medicinal Part: Root.

Actions and Uses: Strengthens kidneys and bladder. Removes excess fluids, gallstones, jaundice and poisons. Excellent for anemia because is high in iron, calcium and other vitamins and minerals. A very good diuretic.

Bodily Influence: Aperient, Deobstruent, Diuretic, Stomachic, and Tonic.

DEVILS CLAW

Medicinal Part: Leaves.

Actions and Uses: A blood cleanser which will remove deposits in the joints and aid in the elimination of uric acid from the body. Very effective for arthritis, gout and rheumatism, as well as liver and kidney disorders.

Bodily Influence: Adaptogen, Alterative, Antirheumatic, and Depurative

DONG QUAI

Medicinal part: Root.

Actions and Uses: Used To treat various female gynecological problems menopause, PMS, and hot flashes. It is the female equivalent of Korean ginseng. Also relieves constipation by moistening the intestinal tract.

Bodily Influence: Adaptogen, Laxiative, and Nutritive.

Warning: Should not be used during pregnancy.

ECHINACEA

Medicinal Parts: Leaves, Dried Rhizome, and Root.

Actions and Uses: Glandular balancer, especially lymphatic and liver areas. Also blood purifier, antiseptic and anti-infection herb. Good for boils, blood poisoning, carbuncles, all pus diseases, snake and spider bites. Helps boost immune response.

Bodily Influence: Alterative, Diaphoretic, and Sialagogue.

Warning: Alcohol tincture may destroy polysaccharides in echinacea that stimulate the immune system.

EVENING PRIMROSE

Medicinal Parts: Bark, Leaves, and Seeds.

Actions and Uses: An excellent source of essential fatty acids (EFA's). Good for skin disorders female disorders such as cramps, hot flashes, heavy bleeding, especially effective against atopic diseases such as eczema, PMS and hyperactivity.

Bodily Influence: Astringent, Nervine, and Sedative

EYEBRIGHT

Medicinal Part: Leaves.

Actions and Uses: It is the main herb for protecting and maintaining the health of the eye. Acts as an internal medicine for the constitutional tendency to eye weakness. Will remove cysts that have been caused by chronic conjunctivitis.

Bodily Influence: Adaptogen, Nutritive.

FENNEL

Medicinal Part: Whole Herb.

Actions and Uses: Helps suppress the appetite. Aids digestion when uric acid is the problem. Good for gas, acid stomach, kidneys, liver, spleen, gout and mixed with catnip in tincture form as an aid to colic in infants. Also relieves pain for cancer patients after chemotherapy and radiation.

Bodily Influence: Antispasmodic, Carmin-ative, and Galactagogue.

FENUGREEK

Medicinal Part: Seeds.

Actions and Uses: Useful for all mucus conditions of the lungs. Good for bronchitis, fevers, sore throats and inflammation of stomach and intestines. Also acts as a bulk laxative.

Bodily Influence: Demulcent, Emollient, Expectorant, and Laxative.

FEVERFEW

Medicinal Parts: Whole Herb.

Actions and Uses: Helpful in the prevention of migraines, relieves dizziness, brain and nerve pressure. Stimulates uterine contractions, promotes menses, increases fluidity of lung and bronchial tube mucus. Also used in alleviating inflammation and discomfort of arthritis and female disorders.

Bodily Influence: Aperient, Carminative, Emmenagogue, Stimulant, Tonic, and Vermifuge.

FO-TI

Medicinal Part: Root.

Actions and Uses: Stimulant, excellent for mental depression. Has been used to help the memory. Recent scientific studies verify cholesterol-lowering effects of this herb. Also helps to rejuvenate the endocrine glands which in turn, strengthen the body.

Bodily Influence: Stimulant and Tonic.

GARLIC

Medicinal Part: Bulb.

Actions and Uses: Natural antibiotic, stimulates activity of the digestive organs,. It is used to emulsify the cholesterol and loosen it from the arterial walls.

Proven useful in asthma and whooping cough. Valuable in intestinal infections and effective in reducing high blood pressure.
Bodily Influence: Alterative, Antibiotic, and Esculent.

GENTAIN

Medicinal Parts: Leaves and Root.
Actions and Uses: Most useful in states of exhaustion from chronic disease, and all cases of general debility, weakness of digestive organs and want of appetite. Kills plasmodia (organisms that cause malaria) and Worms. Many dyspeptic complaints are effectively relieved with gentian.
Bodily Influence: Adaptogen, Fubrifuge, Nutritive, Stimulant, Tonic, and Vermifuge.

GINKGO

Medicinal Part: Leaves.
Actions and Uses: Widens blood vessels, increases circulation and speeds blood flow in the capillaries. Useful for hearing, vision, senility, dizziness, ringing in ears, heart and kidney disorders.
Bodily Influence: Cardiac, Rubifacient, and Vasodilator.

GINGER

Medicinal Part: Root and rhizomes.
Actions and Uses: Hot as tea promotes cleansing of the body through perspiration and useful for suppressed menstruation. Relieves indigestion, gas, morning sickness, nausea. In a recent university study, ginger root capsules proved to be far more effective at controlling motion-induced nausea than either a drug or placebo. It helps absorb toxins, restore gastric activities to normal, and helps control diarrhea and vomiting that often accompanies gastro-intestinal flu.

Bodily Influence: Carminative, Diaphoretic, Diuretic, Stimulant, and Tonic.

GINSENG (KOREAN)

Medicinal Part: Root.
Actions and Uses: A physical restorative. Helps the entire body adapt to stress, regenerates and rebuilds sexual centers. Impotency and low sperm count have been corrected by using Korean Ginseng. Stimulates the appetite, and normalizes blood pressure. Anciently known as a male hormone, and used for longevity.
Bodily Influence: Aphrodisiac, Demulcent, Nervine, Stimulant, and Stomachic.

GINSENG (SIBERIAN)

Medicinal Part: Root.
Actions and Uses: Main action is a tonic and toner of the body, promotes mental and physical vigor, stamina, endurance, metabolism, appetite and digestion. Mildly stimulates the central nervous system, also helpful in problems arising in menopause such as hot flashes and irregular periods. Also good for cocaine withdrawal, radiation protection, and enhances lung, and immune functions.
Bodily Influence: Aphrodisiac, Demulcent, Nervine, Stimulant, and Stomachic.
Caution: Avoid if hyperactive or under high nervous tension.

GOLDEN SEAL HERB

Medicinal Part: Rhizomes.
Actions and Uses: For all problems of the mucus membranes. Contains many of the same properties as the root but in milder form. Relieves nausea. The infusion makes a good vaginal douche.

Bodily Influence: Alterative, Antibiotix, Antiseptic, Emmenagogue, Stomachic, Tonic.
Warning: Do not use large amounts during pregnancy. When used over a long period, will reduce vitamin B absorption.

GOLDEN SEAL ROOT

Medicinal Part: Root.
Actions and Uses: A natural antibiotic herb used with all infections. A powerful agent used in treating ulcers, diphtheria, tonsillitis and spinal meningitis. Combined with Gota Kola, Goldenseal acts as a brain tonic. One of the best substitutes for quinine.
Bodily Influence: Alterative, Antibiotic, Antiseptic, Laxative, and Tonic.

GOTU KOLA

Medicinal Parts: Nuts, Root, and Seeds.
Actions and Uses: Known in India as the longevity herb. Contains remarkable rejuvenating properties. May promote hair growth when combined with eclipta. It strengthens the heart, and liver functions. Good for mental disorders, blood diseases, high blood pressure, sore throat, tonsillitis, hepatitis, measles, rheumatism, and venereal diseases. Used as a brain cell activator to help memory.
Bodily Influence: Antibiotic, Nervine, Rubifacient, and Tonic.

GUAR GUM

Medicinal Part: Leaves And Seed.
Actions and Uses: Used as a diet aid because it absorbs liquids and swells, also reduces serum cholesterol levels and has a mild bulk-forming laxative effect.
Bodily Influence: Esculent, and Laxative.

HAWTHORN

Medicinal Part: Berries and Leaves.
Actions and Uses: A dietary herb, aids in burning off excess calories. Relieves abdominal distention and diarrhea. A herbal aid for circulation and specific nutritional resources for building heart tone. Valuable in angina pectoris or inflammation of the heart muscle.
Bodily Influences: Adaptogen, Cardiac, and Circulatory Tonic.

HOPS

Medicinal Parts: Strobiles or Cones.
Actions and Uses: A powerful sedative, strong yet safe to use. Decreases the desire for alcohol, improves appetite and induces sleep. Good for heart, stomach and liver problems, nervousness, restlessness, pain, toothaches, earaches, and stress.
Bodily Influence: Anodyne, Anthelmintic, Diuretic, Febrifuge, Hypnotic, Nervine, Sedative and Tonic.

HOREHOUND

Medicinal Parts: Whole Herb.
Actions and Uses: Used for congestion of coughs, colds, and pulmonary affections associated with unwanted phlegm from the chest. Good for intestinal gas, when taken in large doses it is a laxative and will expel worms.
Bodily Influence: Anthelmintec, Diuretic, Diaphoretic, Expectorant, Laxative, Resolvent, Stimulant, Stomachic, and Tonic.

HORSETAIL (SHAVEGRASS)

Medicinal Parts: Leaves and Stems.

109

Actions and Uses: Contains a great deal of silica. Increases calcium absorption, promotes healthy skin, strengthens bone, hair, nails, and teeth. Also a diuretic. Helps with kidney disorders, especially kidney stones. Used as poultice to depress bleeding and accelerate healing of wounds.
Bodily Influence: Astringent, Diuretic, Lithotriptic, and Tonic.

HUCKLEBERRY

Medicinal Parts: Whole Plant.
Actions and Uses: Used to lower insulin, blood sugar levels, and to ease inflammation. Good for diabetes, kidney, bladder, sinusitis, and ulcers.
Bodily Influences: Alterative, Depurative, Nutritive, and Stomachic. Caution: Interferes with iron absorption when taken internally.

IRISH MOSS

Medicinal Parts: Whole Plant.
Actions and Uses: Used in cosmetics to soften and promote elasticity of the skin. Also effective in the treatment of thyroid problems (goiter), colon disorders, and obesity.
Bodily Influences: Adaptogen, and Emollient.

JUNIPER BERRY

Medicinal Part: Ripe dry berries.
Actions and Uses: Useful in digestive problems, gastrointestinal infections, inflammations, cramps, dropsy kidney, and bladder diseases. Also good for gout, and other arthritic conditions associated with acid waste.
Bodily Influence: Carminative, Diuretic, and Stimulant.
Warning: Not intended for use during pregnancy.

KAVA KAVA

Medicinal Part: Root.
Actions and Uses: An excellent herb for insomnia and nervousness. Invokes sleep and relaxes the nervous system.
Bodily Influence: Antiseptic, Anti-spasmodic, and Diuretic.
Warning: Long term usage of high dosages can interfere with elimination of toxins from the liver.

KELP (NORWEGIAN)

Medicinal Part: Leaves
Actions and Uses: Source of olkaki, calcium, sulphur, iodine, silicon and vitamin k. Beneficial to reproductive organs and tones the walls of the blood vessels. Excellent for the thyroid gland and goiters. Has a remedial and normalizing action on the sensory nerves. Good for nails, hair, and radiation poisoning.
Bodily Influence: Demulcent, Thyroid restorative, and Nutritive.

LADY SLIPPER ROOT

Medicinal Part: Root.
Actions and Uses: Acts as a tonic to the exhausted nervous system, improving circulation and nutrition of the nerve centers. This in turn calms nerves, mental irritation and quiets spasms of voluntary muscles with no harmful or narcotic effects.
Bodily Influence: Antiperiodic, Nervine, and Tonic.

LICORICE ROOT

Medicinal Part: The dried root.
Actions and Uses: Hormone balancer. Natural cortisone. Used for hypoglycemia, adrenal glands, stress, female problems (menstrual and menopause). Muscle or skeletal spasms, and increases fluidity of mucus from the lungs

and bronchial tubes. Used for coughs, chest complaints, gastric ulcers, and throat conditions.

Bodily Influence: Demulcent, Expectorant, Laxative, and Pectoral.

Warning: Large doses of licorice root should be avoided by people with high blood pressure.

LOBELIA

Medicinal Parts: Leaves, Flower, Seeds and Stem.

Actions and Uses: A powerful relaxant used extensively for persons wishing to stop smoking or drinking. Aids in Hormone production. Reduces palpitation of the heart and strengthens muscle action. Good for fevers, pneumonia, meningitis, pleurisy, hepatitis and peritonitis. The Indians used Red Lobelia for syphilis and for expelling or destroying intestinal worms. Emetic in large amounts.

Bodily Influence: Antispasmodic, Diaphoretic, Emetic, Expectouant, Nauseant, Relaxant, Sedative, and Stimulant.

MARSHMALLOW

Medicinal Parts: Whole Herb.

Actions and Uses: Useful in inflammation and irritation of the alimentary canal, urinary and respiratory organs. Also used in combination with other diuretic herbs during kidney treatment to assist in release of stones.

Bodily Influence: Demulcent, and Emollient.

MILK THISTLE

Medicinal Parts: Fruit, Leaves and Seeds.

Actions and Uses: Regenerates liver cells and protects them against the action of liver poisons (leukotrienes). Beneficial to those with psoriasis. Aids rehabilitation process after acute hepatitis, gall bladder disease or exposure to alcohol, drug or chemical pollution

Bodily Influence: Cholagogue, Liver Tonic.

MILKWEED

Medicinal Part: Root.

Actions and Uses: Used for inflammatory rheumatism, dyspepsia and scrofulous conditions of the blood. A helpful remedy for bowel, kidney, and stomach complaints. Good for female complaints, asthma, arthritis, and bronchitis. Remedy for gall-stones and used for dropsy as it increases the flow of urine.

Bodily Influence: Diaphoretic, and Expectorant.

Warning: May be harmful to children and people over 55.

MULLEIN

Medicinal Parts: Leaves and Flowers.

Actions and Uses: Pain reliever, glandular rebuilder. The only herb known that is a narcotic without being harmful or poisonous. Good for coughs, colds, hay fever, shortness of breath and hemorrhages in lungs. Also used as a treatment for hemorrhoids.

Bodily Influence: Anodyne, Antispasmodic, Astringent, Demulcent, Diuretic, and Pectoral.

MYRRH GUM

Medicinal Part: Leaves.

Actions and Uses: Stimulator, appetite and flow of gastric juices. A powerful antiseptic which is generally used in equal parts with golden seal for intestinal ulcer, catarrh of the intestines and other mucus membrane conditions. Also used for bronchial and lung diseases. Tightening the gums and preventing pyorrhea is one of its most outstanding qualities.

Bodily Influence: Antiseptic, Digestive Aid, and Stimulant.

NETTLE

Medicinal Parts: Roots and Leaves.

Actions and Uses: Tradition use, asthma relief, also used for kidney diseases, colon and urinary disorders, checking hemorrhage of uterus, nose, lungs and other internal organs. Nettle is valuable in diarrhea, dysentery, piles, neuralgia, gravel, and tea made from the young or dried root is of great help in dropsy of the first stages.

Bodily Influence: Astringent, Diuretic, Pectoral, and Tonic.

External Use: Cleansing wounds and ulcers.

OAT BRAN

Medicinal Part: Seed.

Actions and Uses. Contains soluble and insoluble fiber, which have cholesterol-lowering benefits. Also useful in maintaining a healthy colon.

Bodily Influence: Adaptogen and Esculent.

OREGON GRAPE

Medicinal Part: Fruit.

Actions and Uses: Blood purifier and liver activator. Builder of the reproductive organs. Increases the power of digestion and aids assimilation. Recommended as an alternative for treatment of psoriasis, syphilis and unpure blood conditions. Combine with Cascara Sagrada for constipation.

Bodily Influence: Alterative, Esculent, and Tonic.

PARSLEY

Medicinal Parts: Leaves, Seeds, and Root.

Actions and Uses: Rich in vitamin B and potassium. An excellent diuretic, and one of the most excellent herbs for gall bladder problems. Expels gall-stones. Also good for bed wetting, edema, fluid retention, goiter, gas, indigestion, menstrual disorders, and worms. Also useful as a preventative in treating Epilepsy.

Bodily Influence: Anthelmintic, Aperient, Carminative, Diuretic, Esculent, Expectorant and Stimulant.

Caution: Shouldn't be used if the kidney is inflamed. Avoid heavy consumption during pregnancy.

PASSION FLOWER

Medicinal Parts: Plant and Flower.

Actions and Uses: When in need of help for nervousness, unrest, agitation and exhaustion without pain, such as unrest, agitation, and exhaustion, Passion Flower is helpful. Also used to control convulsions, particularly in the young, as indicated by muscular twitching, and also for asthenic insomnia in childhood and the elderly;

Bodily Influence: Anodyne, Antispasmodic, Diuretic, and Nerve Sedative.

PAU D'ARCO

Medicinal Parts: Inner Bark.

Actions and Uses: Undoutably the greatest treasure the Incas left us. Medical literature confirms that this South American herb possesses antibiotic, tumor inhibiting, virus killing, anti fungal, and anti-malarial properties. Consumer publications report success for the symptoms of anemia, asthma, candida, psoriasis, colitis, and resistance to various infections by building the immune system. Due to genetic mutation resistant strains of candida develop rapidly. Patients who no longer respond to Pau d'Arco will find that rotating treatment with Mathake tea to be beneficial.

Bodily influence: Adaptogen, Antibiotic, Nutritive, and Resolvent.

PENNYROYAL

Medicinal Parts: Whole Plant:
Actions and Uses: Diuretic, corrective nervine used to induce perspiration and promote menstruation. Purifies the blood, stimulates uterine contractions, relieves gas and intestinal pains. Also for nervousness and hysteria, cramps, gout, colic, jaundice, nausea, griping, colds. and skin disorders.
Bodily Influence: Corrective, Diaphoretic, Diuretic, and Nervine.
WARNING: Do not use during pregnancy.

PEPPERMINT

Medicinal Parts: Flowers and Leaves:
Actions and Uses: Irritates the gastrointestinal tract, mucous membranes, and increases stomach acidity. Used to relieve gas pains, nausea, dysentery, diarrhea and stop vomiting. Also good for chills, colic, fevers, dizziness, influenza and palpitation of the heart.
Bodily Influence: Adaptogen, Antacid, Carminative, cariac, and Pectoral.
Warning: May interfere with Iron absorption.

PLANTAIN

Medicinal Parts: Whole Plant:
Actions and Uses: Influences lymphatic system and builds tissue. Excellent remedy for kidney and bladder problems. Also used externally on inflamed skin with malignant ulcers, external hemorrhaging, insect bites, burns, scalds and ulcers.
Bodily Influence: Alterative, Antiseptic, Astringent, and Diuretic.

POTENCY WOOD

Medicinal Parts: Root:
Actions and Uses: This herb is used to as a remedy for treating sexual debility and impotency. It regenerates and rebuilds sexual centers, and increases sperm production.
Bodily Influence: Adaptogen, Digestive, Nervine, Nutritive, Stimulant, and tonic.

PROPOLIS

Bees manufacture propolis to prevent disease from entering the hive. As it is a natural antibiotic it wards off all kinds of infections such as colds, flu, fevers, digestive disorders, etc.

PSYLLIUM

Medicinal Part: Seed.
Actions and Uses: Psyllium assists in easy evacuation by increasing water in the colon, cleans out compacted pockets thereby making bowel movements easier for people with colitis and hemorrhoids. Creates bulk. Relieves auto-intoxication.
Bodily Influence: Demulcent, and Laxative.
Warning: Because Psyllium forms an indigestible mass, it should be taken at different times than other supplements.

PUMPKIN

Medicinal Part: Seed and Husks.
Actions and Uses: Used for worms, stomach problems, morning sickness, nausea, and toning the prostate gland.
Bodily Influence: Adaptogen, Anthelmintic, Nervine, and Vermifuge.

PUNCTURE VINE

Medicinal Part: Seed and Husks.

Actions and Uses: This herb is called the natural Viagra. It rebuilds sexual centers and increases sperm production. Studies show that it can increase the testosterone levels by as much as 90%.

Bodily Influence: Adaptogen, Digestive, Nervine, Nutritive, Stimulant and Tonic.

QUEEN OF MEADOW

Medicinal Part: Root.

Actions and Uses: One of the best known herbs for kidney and bladder infections. Valuable in diarrhea, especially for children. Imparts to the bowels some nourishment as well as an astringency.

Bodily Influences: Antacid, Carminative, Demulcent, and Diuretic.

RED CLOVER

Medicinal Part: Blossoms, and Leaves..

Actions and Uses: An excellent blood purifier, glandular restorer and mineralize. Contains silica and other earthy salts. Good for tuberculoses and to fight other bacteria, inflamed lungs, whooping cough, gout, and arthritis. Relaxing to nerves and entire system. Also used for many years as an antidote to cancer.

Bodily Influence: Adapogen, Alterative, Antibiotic, Discutient, Nutritive, Sedative, and Tonic.

RED RASPBERRY

Medicinal Parts: Whole plant.

Actions and Uses: Effective in menstrual problems, decreasing the blood flow without stopping it abruptly. Promotes healthy nails, bones, teeth, and skin. Remedy for dysentery and diarrhea in infants. Tea excellent for morning sickness in pregnancy. Helps prevent miscarriage, and strengthens uterine walls prior to giving birth.

Long-term usage may be required to achieve optimal results.

Bodily Influence: Astringent, Stimulant, and Tonic.

Warning: May interfere with iron absorption.

RESHI MUSHROOM

Medicinal Part: Top.

Actions and Uses: Has a positive effect on the immune system. Good for allergies and auto- immune diseases. Acts as an immune modulator. Has a reported anti-tumor activity. Aids the liver and is helpful for digestion. Has antibacterial and anti viral properties. It has been used for bronchitis, coronary disease, senility and general debility. Used in recent years to treat patients suffering with AIDS.

Bodily Influence: Adaptogen, Alterative, Demulcent, Dicsutient, Esculent, Nutritive, and Tonic.

RHUBARB

Medicinal Part: Root.

Actions and Uses: Useful for colon, spleen, and liver disorders. Enhances gallbladder functions and has a positive effect on duodenal ulcers. Good for headaches, constipation, diarrhea, and hemorrhoids.

Bodily Influence: Adaptogen, Antibiotic, Hepatic, and Stomachic

ROSEHIPS

Medicinal Part: Seed and Pod.

Actions and Uses: An extremely high source of Vitamin C. Thus effective with colds, diarrhea, coughs, consumption, dysentery and scurvy. Also helps to combat stress.

Bodily Influence: Adaptogen, Antiseptic, and Nervine.

SAFFRON

Medicinal Part: Leaves and Root.

Actions and Uses: A natural hydrochloric acid (utilizes sugar of fruits/oils), thus helping arthritics get rid of the uric acid which holds the calcium deposited in joints. Also reduces lactic acid build up.
Bodily Influence: Antacid, Antirheumatic.

SAFFLOWER

Medicinal Part: Flowers.
Actions and Uses: This herb is recommended to soothe the nerves in cases of hysteria. Safflower tea produces perspiration and is used during colds, flu, and fevers.
Bodily Influence: Diaphoretic, Emmenagogue, and Laxative.

SAGE

Medicinal Part: leaves.
Actions and Uses: Best known effect is the reduction of perspiration and stopping the flow of milk in a nursing mother. Also used for nervous conditions, trembling, depression and vertigo.
Bodily Influence: Astringent, Diaphoretic, Expectorant, and Tonic.

SANDALWOOD

Medicinal Part: Stem.
Actions and Uses: The wood yields a medicinal oil used to treat acne, skin diseases, dysentery, and gonorrhea. It is also considered an excellent sedating agent.
Bodily Influence: Antibacterial and Sedative.

SANICLE -SNAKEROOT

Medicinal Parts: Root and Leaves.
Actions and Uses: Possesses powerful cleansing and healing properties both internally and externally. Good for asthma, boils, debility diabetes, diarrhea, gastritis, dysentery, intermittent fevers, lungs, intestines, ozaena, reproductive organs, renal tract, and throat discomfort.
Bodily Influence: Alterative, Anodyne, Astringent, Discutient, Nervine, and Vulnerary.

SARSAPARILLA

Medicinal Part: Root.
Actions and Uses: Widely used by athletes as a natural steroid and as a source of precursors of muscle building hormones. Clears skin disorders such as eczema, and psoriasis. Increases energy, and protects against harmful radiation. Eliminates poisons from the blood and helps cleanse the system of infections. Useful for rheumatism, gout, skin eruptions, ringworm, scrofula, internal inflammation, colds and catarrh.
Bodily Influence: Alterative, Antiscoubutic, Demulcent, Diuretic, and Stimulant.

SAW PALMETTO

Medicinal Part: Berries.
Actions and Uses: A tissue builder. It is recommended in all wasting diseases as it has a marked effect upon all the glandular tissue. Capable of increasing nutrition of the testicles and mamma in functional atony of these organs. Also builds stamina and endurance and rids respiratory membranes of mucus. Also of use in renal conditions and diabetes.
Bodily Influence: Anti-catarrhal, Diuretic, Expectorant, Nutritive, Sedative, and Tonic

SCHIZANDRA FRUIT

Medicinal Part: Root.
Actions and Uses: Used to enhance the immune system. Has an a positive effect on the lungs. Used in some cases for forgetfulness. Also used for insomnia.

Bodily Influence: Adaptogen, Anti-catarrhal, Nervine, and Sedative.

SCULLCAP

Medicinal Part: Whole Herb.
Actions and Uses: A natural anti-depressant. More effective than quinine, and not harmful. Good for neuralgia, aches and pains, rheumatism, convulsions, and nervous tension. Helps reduce high blood pressure, helps heart conditions and disorders of the central nervous systems such as palsy, hydrophobia and epilepsy.
Bodily Influence: Antispasmodec, Nervine, Relaxant, and Restorative.

SENNA

Medicinal Part: Leaves.
Actions and Uses: A stimulant laxative, extremely powerful, should be combined with ginger or fennel to prevent cramping. Will help eliminate most types of worms from the colon if used following wormwood. Use externally for skin diseases and pimples.
Bodily Influence: Cathartic, Laxative, and Vermifuge.
Warning: Do not use during pregnancy or if there is inflammation in intestinal tract.

SHEPHERD PURSE

Medicinal Part: Whole Plant.
Actions and Uses: Controls hemorrhaging of stomach, lungs, uterus and kidneys. Also successfully used in cases of hemorrhaging after childbirth and excessive menstruation. Also valuable when used for dysentery, vulnerary, rheumatism, catarrh, dropsy, and chronic menorrhagia.
External Use: Juice stops external bleeding and heals bruises.
Bodily Influence: Antiscorbutic, Astringent, and Diuretic.

SHITAKI MUSHROOM

Medicinal Part: Top.
Actions and Uses: Used as both food and healing agent in the Orient. Taken to enhance the immune system. Has an anti-tumor activity and helps to enhance the natural protective defenses of the body. Will lower blood cholesterol levels and help to pull fat from the system. May be helpful for those diagnosed with clinical depression.
Bodily Influence: Adaptogen, Discutient, Esculent, Stimulant.

SLIPPERY ELM

Medicinal Part: Inner Bark (fresh or dried).
Actions and Uses: Considered one of the most valuable remedies in herbal practice, having wonderful strengthening and healing qualities. Has a soothing and healing action on all parts it comes in contact with. Used extensively for inflammation of the lungs, bowels, stomach, heart, diseases of female organs, kidney and bladder. Slippery Elm will soothe ulcerated or cancerous stomach when nothing else will.
Bodily Influence: Demulcent, Emollient, and Nutritive.

SOLOMON'S SEAL

Medicinal Part: Rhizome.
Actions and Uses: Helps to mend broken bones. Also pulmonary consumption and bleeding of the lungs, female complaints, bruises, hemorrhoids, inflammations of the stomach, and tumors.
Bodily Influence: Astringent, Demulcent, and Tonic.

ST. JOHN'S WORT

Medicinal Parts: Tops and Flowers.
Actions and Uses: This is one of the most useful of herbs, can be used by young or elderly. Useful

in stopping bed wetting. Also for treatment of dysentery, diarrhea, bleeding of the lungs, worms, jaundice and suppressed urine. Will also correct irregular menstruation.
Bodily Influence: Astringent, Diuretic, Expectorant, Sedative.

STRAWBERRY

Medicinal Part: Leaves, Root and Berries.
Actions and Uses: A good blood purifier, clears eczema and other skin conditions. Very effective in treating intestinal malfunctions (diarrhea, dysentery and weakness of intestines and urinary organs).
Bodily Influence: Mild Astringent, and Diuretic

SQUAW VINE

Medicinal Part: Root.
Actions and Uses: Particularly good for women in building of female organs. It has been used for years by expectant mothers six weeks prior to delivery to aid parturition. Alleviates painful menstruation and is a diuretic. Used for insomnia and also used successfully for gravel and urinary ailments.
Bodily Influence: Adaptogen and Nutritive.

SUMA

Medicinal Parts: Bark, Berries, Leaves, and Roots.
Actions and Uses: Also called Brazilian Ginseng. It is the richest source of naturally-occurring germanium and an immune system booster. It has a positive tonic effect on the endocrine system and helps the body to regulate hormone levels. As a female hormone balancer, Suma will act as a precursor to the production of estrogen if the body needs it. It will not cause the production of more estrogen then

the body can handle. Useful for anemia, diabetes, and stress.
Bodily Influences: Adaptogen, and Tonic.

TEA TREE

Medicinal Part: Leaves.
Actions and Uses: Extremely effective as a germicide and fungicide, the antiseptic power of the Tea Tree Oil is 12 times that of carbolic acid. Good for athletes foot, cold sores, cystitis, dermatitis, wounds, and yeast infections.
Bodily Influence: Antiseptic.

THYME

Medicinal Parts: Whole Plant.
Actions and Uses: Used for hysteria, nervous disorders, fever, headaches, and mucus. Lowers cholesterol levels and is good for sinusitis, asthma, and chronic respiratory problems.
Bodily Influence: Antispasmodic, Carmin-ative, Emmenagogue, and Tonic.

UVA URSI

Medicinal Parts: Leaves.
Actions and Uses: Very useful in diabetes and all kinds of kidney and bladder infections. Helps disorders of the small intestines, spleen, liver, and pancreas. Strengthens heart muscle, and imparts tone to the urinary passages. Excellent remedy for piles, hemorrhoids, kidney stones, and helpful in the treatment of gonorrhea. Also good where there are mucus discharges from the bladder with pus and blood.
Bodily Influence: Adaptogen, Anti-syphilitic, Cardiac, Hemostatic, Stimulant, and Tonic.

VALERIAN ROOT

Medicinal Parts: Root, Rhizomes
Actions and Uses: A strong nervine without a narcotic effect.

117

Soothes and quiets the nervous system, beneficial in cardiac palpitation. Used for epileptic fits, nervous tension or irritations. Excellent for children with measles and scarlet fever.
Bodily Influence: Antispasmodic, Calm-ative, Nervine, Stimulant, and Tonic.

VIOLET

Medicinal Parts: Leaves and Flowers.
Actions and Uses: Useful for pain in cancerous growths. Soothing and healing effect on inflamed mucal surfaces. Good for colds, hoarseness, inflammation of the lungs, and whooping cough.
Externally: Compress on inflamed tumors, sore throat, and swollen breasts.
Bodily Influence: Antiseptic, and Expectorant.

WATER CRESS

Medicinal Parts: Flower, Leaves, and Root.
Actions and Uses: Helps the body to use oxygen, stimulates rate of metabolism, increasing physical endurance and stamina and improves heart response. Used for Bladder, kidney, and liver problems, and dissolves kidney stones.
Bodily Influence: Alterative, Nutritive, Stimulant, and Tonic.

WHITE OAK BARK

Medicinal Parts: Bark and Acorn.
Actions and Uses: Good for varicose veins. Used in douches and enemas, for internal tumors and swellings. Excellent remedy for, hemorrhoids, hemorrhages, varicose veins, tumors, womb troubles, goiter or any trouble of the rectum. Normalizes the liver, kidneys, spleen, and dissolves kidney stones and gallstones.

Bodily Influence: Antiseptic, Astringent Haemostatic, and Tonic.

WHITE WILLOW BARK

Medicinal Part: Bark.
Actions and Uses: It is one of nature's greatest gifts to mankind as a pain-relieving, fever-lowering, anti-inflammatory agent without any side effects. Helps relieve symptoms of headache, fever, arthritis, rheumatism, bursitis, dandruff, eye problems (eyewash), influenza, chills, eczema and nosebleed. Most effective in concentrated extract form.
Bodily Influence: Anodyne, and Astringent.

WILD YAM (DIOSCOREA)

Medicinal Part: Root.
Actions and Uses: Yam is a source of the male sex hormone testosterone and is used for rejuvenating effects. Relieves nauseous symptoms of pregnancy, and will help to prevent miscarriage when combined with ginger. Good for Acne, Angina, Biliousness, Diarrhoea, Dysentery Gall-bladder and Liver disorders.
Bodily Influence: Antispasmodic, Anti-bilious, and Diaphoretic.

WINTERGREEN

Medicinal Part: Whole Plant.
Actions and Uses: Used for centuries for its ability to relieve pains of rheumatism. Also good for headaches, colic, flatulence, gastritis, Neuralgia, pleurodynia, and urinary ailments.
Bodily Influence: Anodyne, Astringent, and Stimulant.

WITCH HAZEL

Medicinal Parts: Bark and Leaves.
Actions and Uses: One of the best known herbs to check internal bleeding, especially for ex-

cessive menstruation, hemorrhages from the lungs, stomach, uterus and bowels. Also useful in reducing pain associated to diarrhea, dysentery and hemorrhoids.
Bodily Influence: Astringent, Sedative, and Tonic.

WOOD BETONY

Medicinal Part: Leaves.
Actions and Uses: Strengthens and stimulates the heart muscle. Expels worms. Good for headache, colic, colds, gout, indigestion, and stomach cramps. Also used for jaundice, Parkinson's disease, and tuberculosis.
Bodily Influence: Anodyne, Antacid, Nutritive, Stomachic, and Vermifuge.

WORM WOOD

Medicinal Parts: Tops and Leaves.
Actions and Uses: Used for aminorrhoes, chronic leucorrhoea, diabetes, diarrhea, female complaints, inflammation of tonsils and quinsy. Also small doses are used for dispersing the yellow bile of jaundice from the skin caused by liver conditions.
Bodily Influence: Anthelmintix, Febuefuge, Narcotic, Stimulant, Stomachic, and Tonic.
Warning: Overdose will irritate the stomach and increase heart action.

YARROW

Medicinal Parts: Whole Herb.
Actions and Uses: Very high in tannic acid thus helps to stop bleeding wounds, hemorrhaging stomach, bowels and lungs. Also useful in menstrual irregularities and has a soothing effect on nervous conditions of the heart.
Bodily Influence: Alterative, Astringent, Diuretic, and Tonic.
Warning: Interferes with the absorption of iron.

YELLOW DOCK

Medicinal Parts: Leaves and Roots.
Actions and Uses: It is a powerful restorer of the lymphatic system. Also a blood purifier, laxative, astringent and effective in skin problems such as psoriasis, eczema, and urticarea. When made into an ointment it is valuable to use for swelling, open sores and itching eruptions. Combine with Sarsaparilla as a tea for chronic skin disorders.
Bodily Influence: Alterative, Antiscorbutic, Astringent, Laxative, and Tonic.

YERBAMATE

Medicinal Parts: Whole Herb.
Actions and Uses: Used to enhance the healing powers of other herbs. Stimulates the mind, and nervous system, retards aging, and stimulates the production of cortisone. Also good for allergies, hay fever, arthritis, fluid retention, and constipation.
Bodily Influences: Adaptogen, Alterative, Anodyne, Antirheumatic, Nervine, and Sedative.

YUCCA

Medicinal Part: Root.
Actions and Uses: New hope for arthritics. Contains special steroid saponins which are effective in treating acute forms of arthritis and rheumatism. Tests at the University of Wyoming show that Yucca may also have an anti-cancer potential.
Bodily Influence: Alterative, Anti-rheumatic, and Disculient.

Vitamin & Herb Guide ...

Homeopathic Singular Tissue Salts
Amino Acid Supplements

L-Arginine Metabolizes body fat and tones muscle tissue, increases sperm count in males, aids in the healing of wounds.

L-Aspartic acid Improves stamina and endurance, increases resistance to fatigue, helps protect the central nervous system.

L-Carnitine Body fat stores by converting nutrients into energy, enhances athletic performance, disperses excess calories.

L-Cystine Helps to detoxify the system, aid in protection from smoke, alcohol and heavy metals, also helps protect the body against x-rays and nuclear radiation.

L-Glutamine Used primarily as a brain fuel (improves intelligence). Alleviates fatigue, and depression, also used in the control of alcoholism.

L-Glycine Used in the treatment of gastric hyperacidity, academia, low pituitary gland function and progressive muscular dystrophy.

L-Lysine Improves concentration and mental alertness. Utilizes fatty acids required in energy production, useful in the control and prevention of herpes simplex infection.

L-Methionine Used in the treatment of edema and some cases of schizophrenia, research indicates a possible link to atherosclerosis and cholesterol deposits.

L-Ornithine Involved in the release of human growth hormone, converts fat into energy and muscle, strengthens immune system, accelerates tissue repair and wound healing.

L-Phenylalanine Controls hunger, improves memory, and alertness, enhances sexual interest, helps alleviate depression.

DL-Phenylalanine A non addictive and non toxic natural pain killer, also is a very strong anti-depressant.

L-Tryptophan Anti-depressant, reduces anxiety, tension and promotes sleep. Lowers pain sensitivity, also aids in the control of alcoholism.

L-Tyrosine Appetite depressant, fights fatigue and depression, helps cocaine addicts kick the habit — alleviates the withdrawal symptoms.

A Word About Tissue Salts

Dr. W. H. Schuessler isolated them in the late nineteenth century. Also known as (Schuessler biochemical cell salts). Tissue salts are inorganic mineral components of your body tissues. Dr. Schuessler found that illness occurred if the body was deficient in any of these salts and the body could heal itself if the deficiency was corrected. We recommend that you use only the dosages prescribed on the manufacturer's label as there is a variant in strengths between different manufacturers.

Homeopathic Singular Tissue Salts

Mineral	Actions & Uses	Affected Components
#1 CALC-FLUOR (Calcium Fluoride) (Fluoride of Lime)	Maintains elasticity of tissues.	Impaired circulation, piles, varicose veins, muscle tendon strain, deficient enamel teeth, carbuncles, cracked skin, and over-relaxed conditions.
#2 CALC-PHOS (Calcium Phosphate) (Phosphate of Lime)	Constituent of bones, teeth, and gastric juices.	Impaired digestion, anemia, cold hands and feet, numbness, hydrocele, teething, sore breasts, and night sweats.
#3 CALC-SULPH (Calcium Sulfate) (Sulfate of Lime)	Blood purifier, constituent of all connective tissue in minute particles.	Acne, skin eruptions, abscesses, pimples during adolescence, sore lips, and chronic oozing ulcers.
#4 FERR-PHOS (Iron Phosphate)	The biochemic first aid oxygenates the blood.	Diarrhea, nosebleeds, coughs, colds, chills, fevers, inflammation, congestion, rheumatic pain, and excessive menses.
#5 KALI-MUR (Potassium Chloride) (Chloride of Potash)	Blood constituent and conditioner. Found in lining under surface body cells.	Coughs, colds, respiratory ailments. also granulation of eyelids, warts, and blistering eczema.

Homeopathic Singular Tissue Salts

Mineral	Actions & Uses	Affected Components
#6 KALI-PHOS (Potassium Phosphate)	Nerve Nutrient. Found in all nerve, brain, and blood cells.	Nervous exhaustion, indigestion, headaches, poor memory, anxiety, insomnia, and improper fat digestion.
#7 KALI-SULPH (Potassium Sulfate) (Sulfate of Potash)	Oxygenates the tissue salts. Constituent 0f skin cells, and internal organ linings.	Pains in limbs, feeling of heaviness, skin eruptions with sealing or sticky exudation, falling hair, and diseased nails.
#8 MAG-PHOS (Magnesium Phosphate) (Phosphate of magnesia)	Nerve stabilizer and anti-spasmodic. Constituent of bones, teeth, brain, nerves, blood, and muscle cells.	Cramps, neuralgia, shooting pains, flatulence, and colic.
#9 NAT-MUR (Sodium Chloride) (Chloride of Soda)	Water-distribution. Regulates the amount of moisture in the body.	Loss of smell or taste, salt cravings, colds, watery discharges from eyes, and nose.
#10 NAT-PHOS (Sodium Phosphate) (Phosphate of Soda)	Acid-neutralizer. Emulsifies fatty acids and keeps uric acid soluble in the blood.	Over acidity of the blood, jaundice, gastric disorders, heartburn, and rheumatic tendency.
#11 NAT-SULPH (Sodium Sulphate) (Sulphate of Soda)	Excess water eliminator. An irritant to tissues and functions as a stimulant for natural secretions.	liver symptoms, gall bladder disorders, edema, depression, low fevers, bilious attacks, and watery infiltration's.
#12 SILICA (Silicic Oxide) (Silicic Acid)	Conditioner, cleanser, eliminator. Constituent of all connective tissue cells.	Lack of luster or falling hair, boils, impure blood, brittle, ribbed or ingrown nails, carbuncles, and poor memory.

Homeopathic Combination Tissue Salts

Combination	Ingredients	Therapeutic Use
A	Ferr Phos, Kali Phos, Mag Phos	Used for neuritis, neuralgia, and sciatica.
B	Calc Phos, Kali Phos, Ferr Phos	Used during convalescence and general debility.
C	Mag Phos, Nat Phos, Nat Sulph, Silica	For acidity, heartburn, and dyspepsia.
D	Kali Mur, Kali Sulph, Calc Sulph, Silica	Acne, eczema, scalp eruptions, and skin ailments.
E	Calc Phos, Mag Phos, Nat Phos, Nat Sulph	For flatulence, colic and indigestion.
F	Kali Phos, Mag Phos, Nat Mur, Silica	For nervous headaches, migraine when associated with nervous weakness.
G	Calc Fluor, Calc Phos, Kali Phos, Nat Mur	For backache, lumbago, piles, and over-relaxed condition of the tissues.
H	Mag Phos, Nat Mur, Silica	Hay fever.
I	Ferr Phos, Kali Sulph, Mag Phos	Fibrosis and muscular pains
J	Ferr Phos, Kali Mur, Nat Mur	A seasonal remedy for coughs and colds.
K	Kali Sulph, Nat Mur, Silica	Falling hair, brittle nails.
L	Calc Fluor, Ferr Phos, Nat Mur	Loss of elasticity of veins and arteries.
M	Nat Phos, Nat Sulph, Kali Mur, Calc Phos	For rheumatism.
N	Calc Phos, Kali Mur, Kali Phos, Mag Phos	For menstrual pain.
P	Calc Fluor, Calc Phos, Kali Phos, Mag Phos	For poor circulation, chilblains, aching legs, and feet.
Q	Ferr Phos, Kali Mur, Kali Sulph, Nat Mur	For sinus disorders.
R	Calc Fluor, Calc Phos, Ferr Phos, Mag Phos, Silica	For infants' teething pain and to aid dentition.
S	Kali Mur, Nat Phos, Nat Sulph	For stomach upset, digestive and intestinal disorders, and headaches.

Herbal glossary

Term		Definition
Adaptogen	—	Balances and restores tone to a particular area
Alterative	—	Promotes cleansing and detoxification of blood.
Anodyne	—	Herb used to ease or relieve pain.
Anthelmintic	—	Used to expel intestinal worms
Antacid	—	Helps regulate acid conditions in the stomach.
Antibilious	—	Acts on the bile, relieving biliousness.
Antibiotic	—	Eradicates viruses and bacteria.
Anticatarrhal	—	Eliminates mucus conditions.
Antiemetic	—	Stops vomiting.
Antileptic	—	Relieves fits.
Antiperiodic	—	Arrests morbid periodic movements.
Antipyretic	—	Cools system reducing fevers.
Antirheumatic	—	Relieves or cures rheumatism.
Antiscorbutic	—	Cures or prevents scurvy.
Antiseptic	—	Helps prevent putrefaction.
Antispasmodic	—	Relieves or prevents spasms.
Antisyphilitic	—	Having affect or curing venereal diseases.
Carminative	—	Expels gas from the bowels.
Cardiac	—	Pertaining to or affecting the heart.
Carthartic	—	Cause evacuating from the bowels.
Cephalic	—	Remedies used in diseases of the head.
Cholagogue	—	Increases the flow of bile.
Condiment	—	Improves the flavor of food.
Demulcent	—	Soothing, relieves internal inflammation.
Deobstruent	—	Removes obstructions.
Depurative	—	Purifies the blood.
Detergent	—	Cleansing to boils, ulcers and wounds, etc.
Diaphoretic	—	Produces and increases perspiration.
Discutient	—	Dissolves and heals tumors, abnormal growths.
Diuretic	—	Increases the secretion and flow of urine.
Emetic	—	Induces vomiting.
Emmenagogue	—	Promotes and stimulates menstrual flow.

The Natural Choice...

Term		Definition
Emollient	—	Softens, soothes inflamed tissue.
Esculent	—	Eatable as a food.
Exanthematous	—	Remedy for skin eruptions and diseases.
Expectorant	—	Expulsion of phlegm from mucus membrane.
Febrifuge	—	Abates and reduces fevers.
Galactagogue	—	Promotes secretion of breast milk.
Hemostatic	—	Agent that arrests internal bleeding.
Hepatic	—	For liver diseases, stimulates secretive functions.
Herpatic	—	A remedy for skin diseases of all types.
Laxative	—	Promotes bowel action.
Lithontryptic	—	Dissolves and discharges calculi in urinary organs.
Lymphatic	—	Used to stimulate and cleanse lymphatic system.
Maturating	—	Ripens or brings boils to a head.
Mucilaginous	—	Soothing to all inflammation.
Nauseant	—	Produces vomiting.
Nervine	—	Acts on nervous system, stops nervous excitement.
Nutritive	—	Supplies nutrients, aids building and toning body.
Opthalmicum	—	A remedy for the healing of eye diseases.
Parasiticide	—	Kills and expels parasites from the skin.
Parturient	—	Induces and promotes labor at childbirth.
Pectoral	—	A remedy for chest affections.
Precursor	—	Starts a chain reaction which accelerates growth.
Purgative	—	Causes copious excretions from the bowels.
Refrigerant	—	Cooling.
Resolvent	—	Dissolves boils and tumors.
Rubifacient	—	Increases circulation and produces red skin.
Sedative	—	Nerve tonic, relieves excitement, promotes sleep.
Sialogogue	—	Increases the secretion of saliva.
Stimulant	—	Increases energy, assists functional activity.
Stomachic	—	Strengthens, tones stomach. Relieves indigestion.
Styptic	—	Contracts tissues, blood vessels, arrests bleeding.
Sudorific	—	Produces profuse perspiration.
Tonic	—	A remedy which is invigorating and strengthening.
Vermifuge	—	Destroys and expels worms from the system.
Vulnerary	—	Promotes healing by stimulating cell growth.

Global Health Research Books are available directly from the publishers.
Send list price plus $2.50 for shipping and handling.

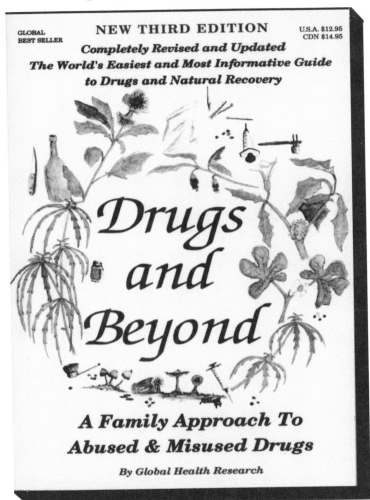

GLOBAL BEST SELLER

NEW THIRD EDITION

U.S.A. $12.95
CDN $14.95

Completely Revised and Updated
The World's Easiest and Most Informative Guide
to Drugs and Natural Recovery

Drugs and Beyond

A Family Approach To Abused & Misused Drugs

By Global Health Research

Over 700,000 Copies Sold
A family approach to abused and misused drugs.

This is an informative, heavily researched book which has been written to help you fully understand drugs, their uses and how they affect you and your family. **It provides** *helpful natural treatments and herbal alternatives* **which aid in recovery for over 120 different abused and misused drugs** and contains the latest up-to-date factual information on drugs and how to recognize the effects of use and/or abuse. It is set up in an easy to use format utilizing questions with explicit answers, and clearly designed charts and diagrams for quick glance information. The information in this book will give a better understanding about what drugs are, why they are used and how we can help diminish their illicit use.

$12.95 U.S.A. - $14.95 Cdn.

Global Health Research Books are available directly from the publishers.
Send list price plus $2.50 for shipping and handling.

INTERNATIONAL BEST SELLER

REVISED 2001 EDITION

U.S.A. $22.95
CDN $29.95

The "Complete" Natural Health Encyclopedia

By David H. Nyholt
Author of the International best selling books
THE VITAMIN & HERB GUIDE and THE ATHLETE'S BIBLE

This concise, comprehensive, and easy to use natural health encyclopedia, is designed to give you more practical information in less reading time. It features the latest breakthroughs in natural health science. Proven and effective natural treatments for over 600 common ailments. 400 western and oriental herbs with their up to date characteristics. 120 Homeopathic remedies. The healing and toxic qualities of 130 foods and spices. Charts on Vitamins, Minerals, Amino Acids, Tissue Salts, and the recommended daily allowances. A must for all people wishing to restore health and prevent premature aging.

The Natural Health Encyclopedia by David Nyholt --- $22.95 U.S.A./$29.95 Cdn.

Global Health Research Books are available directly from the publishers.
Send list price plus $2.50 for shipping and handling.

BEST
GLOBAL
SELLER

THE
ATHLETES
BIBLE

A COMPLETE GUIDE TO

SUPPLEMENTS

BUILDER OF CHAMPIONS

AMINOS ———— STEROIDS
STEROLS ———— VITAMIN PAKS
CARBS ———— PROTEINS
HIGH ENERGY & INJURY FIGHTING
SUPPLEMENTS

HOW TO USE – WHAT TO EXPECT

Over 500,000 Copies Sold

The proper nutrition to boost your athletic abilities.

If you are a Olympic, professional, or recreational athlete, this is the book for you.
Concise, up to date information on high performance sport nutrition, aminos, ster
oids, sterols, vitamins, carbs, proteins, high energy and injury fighting supple
ments. enables you to boost your athletic abilities, promote safe muscle tissue
growth, increase strength and stamina. Enhance energy levels through proper
nutritional supplementation and reach your highest possible potential, withou
harmful drugs or chemical additives.

The Athletes Bible by David Nyholt
$9.95 U. S. - $11.95 Cdn.